Praise for *To Write As If*

"This book is a tour de force. I was completely awestruck by the way Zambreno enacts the concept of the title, and by the way she writes the body, hers and Guibert's. It is a moving performative act, a document of our time from the trenches, and a brilliant critical study."

—MOYRA DAVEY, AUTHOR OF *INDEX CARDS: SELECTED ESSAYS*

"The transgressive novelist and first significant memoirist of life with AIDS, Hervé Guibert was, by the time he died, expert at turning a book into a time bomb and vice versa. Thirty years later, against a backdrop of inequities exposed by the coronavirus public health crisis and amid her own ticking biology and professional precarity, Kate Zambreno considers the composite of guile and candor and care and betrayal that is high-stakes life-writing, itself perhaps a 'virus that "preys on the human propensity to connect."' The result is Zambreno's most urgent and charged work since *Heroines*."

— BRIAN BLANCHFIELD, AUTHOR OF *PROXIES: ESSAYS NEAR KNOWING*

"Kate Zambreno's *To Write As If Already Dead* is portrait and self-portrait. It's a book about friendship, or friendships— famous, fictional, friends we've had and lost. More than this, it's about what it means to feel kinship with a particular book and writer, and so it's really about reading, that intimacy and solitude. Here, as ever, Zambreno proves herself a brilliantly generous and ambitious reader, one capable of engaging a text so acutely that the line between self and art blurs. *To Write As If Already Dead* is gossipy and smart, angry and agile, doubling and doubled—and a serious pleasure to read."

— DANIELLE DUTTON, AUTHOR OF
MARGARET THE FIRST

"Kate Zambreno stylizes a thrilling form of reading as writing and writing as reading, one that speaks to the overlapping crises of our contemporary moment in tones compelling, honest, and withering in all the right ways. No one thinks better and more carefully about the embodied practice of writing. She is the only person who could have written this book."

— AMY HOLLYWOOD, AUTHOR OF *ACUTE MELANCHOLIA
AND OTHER ESSAYS*

"More provocation than evocation, Kate Zambreno's *To Write As If Already Dead* treats Hervé Guibert's life and work as an urgent, at-times vexing ethical and moral code by which life and literary achievement might be measured. Zambreno does much more than 'closely' read; she establishes a radical intimacy between author, subject, and reader, one built of contradiction and continuity. Here, Guibert's voice is restored to the present through an act of transportation that left me slightly afraid of Zambreno's power. But then that's why you read her, and him: for a new awe of life."

— ANDREW DURBIN, AUTHOR OF *SKYLAND*

To Write As If Already Dead

REREADINGS

EDITED BY NICHOLAS DAMES AND JENNY DAVIDSON

Short and accessible books by scholars, writers, and critics, each one revisiting a favorite post-1970 novel from the vantage point of the now. Taking a look at novels both celebrated and neglected, the series aims to display the full range of the possibilities of criticism, with books that experiment with form, voice, and method in an attempt to find different paths among scholarship, theory, and creative writing.

To Write As If Already Dead

Kate Zambreno

COLUMBIA UNIVERSITY PRESS

New York

Columbia University Press
Publishers Since 1893
New York   Chichester, West Sussex
cup.columbia.edu

Library of Congress Cataloging-in-Publication Data
Names: Zambreno, Kate, author.
Title: To write as if already dead / Kate Zambreno.
Description: New York : Columbia University Press, [2021]
Identifiers: LCCN 2020058121 (print) |
LCCN 2020058122 (ebook) | ISBN 9780231188449 (hardback ;
acid-free paper) | ISBN 9780231188456 (trade paperback ;
acid-free paper) | ISBN 9780231547857 (ebook)
Classification: LCC PS3626.A6276 T6 2021 (print) |
LCC PS3626.A6276 (ebook) | DDC 818/.609—dc23
LC record available at https://lccn.loc.gov/2020058121
LC ebook record available at https://lccn.loc.gov/2020058122

Columbia University Press books are printed on permanent and
durable acid-free paper.
Printed in the United States of America

Cover design: Julia Kushnirsky
Cover image: Sarah Charlesworth Skull, 2000
© The Estate of Sarah Charlesworth.
Courtesy of Paula Cooper Gallery, New York.

This is a work of fiction as well as a work of criticism.
In the spirit of Guibert's novel, some liberties have been
taken, and some characters, details, or names are products
of the author's imagination.

CONTENTS

For Bhanu Kapil

To Write As If Already Dead

I

Disappearance

"*In the years of friendship I see those I love in mosaic-like patterns, and me along with them. Who will ever know our names in a hundred years!*"

—Bruce Boone, *Century of Clouds*

There comes a moment when you are finally given some space and quiet, maybe an hour, possibly two, the occasional birdsong by an open window, and you must go to that other room and return to the problem you've been attempting to unravel. It's difficult to believe how much time has passed since you last attempted to work through this problem, this problem which is the problem of a friendship.

The summer weather outside the window in the front room, where my desk now resides, takes me to that small Manet landscape *The Funeral*. Perhaps the mood of the clouds, something of the light. At the foot of the hill, smudges of a wan, black-garbed procession behind a coffin carried by horse and carriage. The dark green brushstrokes of the trees on the hillside. It is a painting that I've thought about for years. A grayscale print-out was once taped to the wall above my desk when it was in the other room. In the past I would pilgrimage to the Met to visit this painting, the baby hanging off me or asleep in her stroller. In the gallery it is dwarfed by Manet's gigantic portraits enthralled to Velázquez and set against dusky backgrounds, the velvety black of the Spanish singer's hat and jacket, the shocking blood of the matador's cape.

The museum has been closed now for months. I think of the paintings hanging there alone, with no one to gaze at them. Are they covered over, like a shroud?

The Funeral is said to depict Charles Baudelaire's funeral on September 2, 1867. The absence of a crowd could possibly be explained by others being away from Paris on holiday, or the threat of the gathering storm. Manet was one of the few mourners present. Although Baudelaire spent his last years in a nursing home in Paris, he had been estranged from the city for some time, in his penurious exile to Belgium. No longer being able to share walks with his friend in the Tuileries, Manet would write complaining about the shocking reception of his paintings in the Salon, which had previously rejected him, how he was savaged and caricatured by the press, both he and his paintings seen as stupid, abominable, ugly. Baudelaire had little patience for his friend's bourgeois craving for approval. One caustic reply, from 1865: "Do you believe you are the first man to find yourself in such a place? Have you more genius than Chateaubriand and Wagner? People mocked them quite a lot don't you know. They did not die from it." The painting was unfinished, only discovered in Manet's studio after his death. I wonder how often he looked at it, and when he did, whether he still thought of his friend. Perhaps it was unfinished because there was something still unsettled, even private, for him about the canvas.

In Hervé Guibert's novel *À l'ami qui ne m'a pas sauvé la vie*, or *To the Friend Who Did Not Save My Life*, his speculative chronology of his own AIDS diagnosis, he writes that after the death of his famous friend Michel Foucault, fictionalized as Muzil, the philosopher's companion, a character closely based on AIDS activist Daniel Defert, placed notices in two newspapers to publicize the ceremonial *levée du corps*, or "raising of the body," when the coffin would be carried out into the courtyard of the Hôpital de la Pitié-Salpêtrière. The worry was that it would be more sparsely attended than the funeral of another famous French intellectual who died a few years earlier, a reference to the death in 1980 of Roland Barthes, who languished in the same hospital for one month, after being run over by a laundry van in the streets of Paris and found on the streets without his identification. In competition even in death, these colleagues at the Collège de France who were both Guibert's mentors, as well as subject to what could be interpreted as his betrayal in print: when Guibert published Barthes's love letter to him in a journal, and then, in the novel, writing about Foucault's sadomasochistic activities and death from a mysterious illness that would later be identified as AIDS. Both died anonymously in the same hospital, the very hospital, originally a women's asylum, within which Foucault centered his history of madness. Anonymously because that is how one dies. And yet others on their behalf sought to ensure a legacy in the form of a large funeral crowd for the two theorists who argued that the author must disappear within their text, first Barthes in 1967's "The Death of the Author," and then Foucault's challenge, two years later, in "What is an Author?" The best distinction I've read between the dueling essays is that Barthes wants to kill the author, Foucault wants the author to take on the appearance of a dead man.

My favorite Manet of his Spanish period isn't at the Met. I've only seen it online—the matador prone on the ground, the sensual black and glaring white tights of his costume, the gorgeous pink scarf spread out in the foreground that matches the cummerbund. *L'Homme Mort*, it is called. *The Dead Man.*

Two years ago, I walked around what I imagined was that same courtyard of La Salpêtrière, foggily trying to think and take photographs, the toddler asleep in the travel stroller, as the point of this trip was ostensibly a pilgrimage, having been under contract for a study of the Guibert novel for two years, ever since the birth of my daughter. I had received a modest amount from the travel fund of the college where I was perpetual guest faculty to partially pay for my trip to London for a panel on "Writing the Body" at a feminist book fair. The child would fly free for one more month. We would then take the high-speed train to Paris, her father would have the two-year-old by himself for an afternoon so I could think about Guibert, maybe write some notes towards the project. At least that was the idea. It never happened. We spent most of our limited time in Paris traveling to playgrounds and carousels to entertain our jet-lagged child who we plied with large quantities of chocolate mousse and croissants in order to satiate her before taking her to museums, although she still threw a sugar-spiked tantrum at the Franz West show at the Pompidou, while crawling all over his goopy pastel couch-sculptures, then finally passing out nearby at an outdoor café in her plastic-shrouded stroller in the rain as her father and I picked at our food, experiencing that bone-level exhaustion we have only known since becoming parents.

Two days earlier, in London, just as we were going to be separated for the event at the Barbican, I had to calm her down by nursing her in the museum restaurant's narrow bathroom stall, her standing up between my legs on the toilet, while with my spare hand I wrote Bhanu that, of course, this was how I was able to prepare for a panel on "Writing the Body," my first event ever abroad, nursing my daughter melting down in a toilet stall. At the event, after listening to a panelist describe her close intergenerational bonds, the way she was able to discuss her body openly with her mother and grandmother, I then told the story of being about 7 or

8 years old, and my mother placing on my sister's bed in the room we shared together a library book detailing the female reproductive system and the process of menstruation, and then closing the door, this being the last I would hear from her on these subjects, sexual education delegated to segregated classrooms taught by a nun and priest respectively, the major lesson being not to do it, and if you did, never get an abortion. I remember now, it was while in Paris I got my first period in two years, the first since being pregnant, and secretly hoped it was implantation bleeding instead, which would mean I was pregnant yet again, although I met this possible news simultaneously with dread, dread for actually having another child, or going through the waves of suffering again, it was uncertain to me.

All I could think while walking away from the hospital, us managing to buy sandwiches and an apple tart at a nearby stand, was that Foucault and Barthes died next door to the Gare d'Austerlitz, which made me wonder if I was in a Sebaldian mystery, except of course not alone. We had taken the taxi that morning to the Jardin des Plantes nearby, and, unable to even stop and look at the garish cluster of statue like flamingoes while circling around the menagerie, I thought blearily of Rilke staring at the panther behind the bars at that same zoo, more than a century earlier, musing at the trapped animal's existential state, as I was thinking about Rilke for my novel. The opening of Sebald's *Austerlitz* features a narrator exhausted by walking circles around Antwerp, taking refuge on the bench besides the aviary. The blinking eyes of the owls in the Nocturama are confused for him with the vision of travelers in the waiting room at the train station where he meets the fictional character Jacques Austerlitz, modeled on Walter Benjamin, the cut-out gaze of Ludwig Wittgenstein staring out from the page.

Never alone except in writing, and not even then. Recently, up
in the middle of the night, unable to go back to sleep, I begin to
reread Roland Barthes's "The Death of the Author"— "no one of
which is original: the text is a tissue of citations." I always envied
writers who were able to get real work done by foregoing sleep.
Especially writers who are mothers, like Sofia who gets up before
dawn to read, to have any space for solitude, to be her own self.
And yet also, the beauty of not existing in those early hours,
except for the sound of the fans and the occasional car on the
street. Lately Sofia and I write each other what we're reading, if
we've been able to read, a barometer for both of us of having time
and space, as well as our well-being. Sometimes this is all we will
write to each other, not knowing what else to write, through the
exhaustion of the current moment. Often lately, I'm not reading
anything new, except I'm attempting my one or two hours a day,
often cut up throughout the day, to think about Hervé Guibert,
I write Sofia. She tells me she's been trying to get through Baudelaire's essays. I wonder now if she was reading his lectures about
art written while self-exiled in Brussels, hoping to eventually be
paid to do a circuit like his idol Edgar Allen Poe in America, a
period in his life that Sofia and I have discussed before, because
of my fascination with how writers have historically made money,
and when this desire is expressed nakedly, how it affects the form.
Baudelaire loathed Belgium, he wrote that the people were loud,
horrible, grotesque, as well as smelly, there was no art or philoso-
phy, in short, Belgium was a monster. The survival energy running through these last years, escaping creditors, estranged from
his friends, like Guibert isolating himself in Rome and then Elba,
while wrestling with and writing through his diagnosis. The signs
of Baudelaire's deterioration over a decade, in 1855 Nadar photographs the poet still rakish in his peacoat, although the effects of
his poverty and laudanum abuse are beginning to surface on his

face, but by the time he sits for a portrait by Etienne Carjat in 1863, in his floppy silk bowtie, he is slumped over, tight-lipped, sullen, his heavy drinking and opium addiction accelerating his aging, an elderly man at 42, the age I am while writing this. Two years later, in 1865, Carjat takes the final portrait of the poet in Paris, his hair grayer and swept back, his gaze steady. It is strange how often Baudelaire consented to posing for photographs, despite his scorn for the medium, once writing that, "I consider it useless and tedious to represent what exists, because nothing that exists satisfies me. Nature is ugly, and I prefer the monsters of my fantasy to what is positively trivial." Perhaps this is why he looks so furious in that one Carjat photograph—it's like he is saying, just take my fucking photograph already and be done with it.

I am reminded of the tension between Foucault the televisual celebrity, the iconography of his bare-headed visage, and the Foucault who desired to be like the faceless philosopher Maurice Blanchot, whose dinner invitation he turned down, as an homage to him, saying he knew the writings, there was no need to know the author. There is that iconic portrait of Foucault, taken by Guibert in 1981, three years before Foucault's death, before Guibert would write about him in his novel. It was Guibert who once said that he felt closer to betraying his friends when photographing them, rather than when he wrote about them. Perhaps because when one writes it becomes language, so already a strange, skewed space, the realm of fiction. Also being photographed is an alienating process, especially for an intellectual, to be reduced to surface, the "kind of vertigo, something of a 'detective anguish'" that Barthes writes about when considering his own author portrait in *Camera Lucida*, his amnesia as to when the photograph was ever taken in conflict with the reality in front of him. In Guibert's portrait of his friend, Foucault stands at the center of a doorway, outfitted in a kimono, his arms behind his back, his repeated reflection in a set of mirrors, including the door. The neutral expression on his face, although it's an intimate portrait, he looks at the camera with the amused gaze of a friend.

Something of the multiplicity of the photograph resembles the opening movement or frontispiece of Muzil's portrait in *To the Friend*, which reads like a series of folds or curtains. The narrator tells the story of Muzil strategically choosing seating at a restaurant that would allow his back to be to the crowd while also avoiding facing any mirrors. "The public would see only the gleaming and self-contained enigma of that skull he took care to shave every morning." There is the anecdote about the doctor seen before the narrator's diagnosis, one Dr. Nacier, specialist in geriatrics, who wishes to approach Muzil about financing for a nursing home, a form of "designer death resort." Muzil finds this perversely hilarious, and instead suggests that the nursing home should be where people only pretend to die:

> Everything there should be luxurious, with fancy paintings and soothing music, but it would all just be camouflage for the real mystery, because there'd be a little door hidden away in a corner of the clinic, perhaps behind one of those dreamily exotic pictures, and to the torpid melody of a hypodermic nirvana, you'd secretly slip behind the painting, and presto, you'd vanish, quite dead in the eyes of the world, since no one would see you reappear on the other side of the wall, in the alley, with no baggage, no name, no nothing, forced to invent a new identity for yourself.

While reading this I realize that the passage mirrors Foucault's reading of the *mise en abyme* in Velázquez's *Las Meninas*, which opens *The Order of Things*. The mysterious void behind the painting within the painting. The space beyond the space of the picture, that the picture can only suggest in a glimpse, an almost hidden, possible other world. André Gide writing of the desire for a *mise en abyme* in writing. A book within a book. A copy within a copy. An infinite reoccurrence. Both passages also echoing Foucault's "What is an Author?", which reads like a noir. "Rather, it is primarily concerned with creating an opening where the writing subject endlessly disappears." Foucault, renamed Muzil by Guibert in a nod to his famous friend's desire to be a man without qualities, to vanish behind the curtain, also perhaps a nod to Robert Musil's masterwork being unfinished, which mirrors Foucault's own unfinished multivolume history of sexuality. In Guibert's novel, a hospital visitor tries to talk to Muzil about an unnamed master painting recently exhibited in the Grand Palais, a reference to Foucault's ekphrasis of *Las Meninas*, and Muzil has no idea what he's talking about, and then worries that he is losing his mind, or at the least his memory. Baudelaire spent his final two years in a nursing home, aphasic and paralyzed from a stroke. Entirely divorced from language—the cruelest ending for such a poet. I read somewhere that in his last days, in his aphasic state, he called out for Manet. Apparently his last words were repeating *"Cré nom!"* or "Holy shit!" over and over.

"Don't pull the Max Brod-Kafka trick on me," a dying Foucault reportedly scolded friends, regarding his will stipulating no posthumous publication, which was ultimately unheeded, just as Kafka's literary executor ignored his friend's desire to destroy his archive after his death. In the novel, Muzil finds and destroys his in-progress manuscript on Manet, as well as ultimately all of his unfinished manuscripts, after the Guibert narrator requests a copy in order to work on a kindred study, also never finished, entitled *The Painting of the Dead*. Years later, once the narrator is exiled in Rome, writing this novel, his lover Jules suggests that he take up painting, worried about his mental health following his diagnosis (Jules is based on Guibert's longtime lover and frequent photography subject Thierry Journo, who keeps the name across the late illness cycle. In real life Guibert was in Rome for a two-year writing residency at the Villa Médicis from 1987–1989, along with his friend Mathieu Lindon.) Instead, while flipping through a catalogue in a bookstore, Guibert's narrator becomes obsessed with the mystery behind a reproduction of the 1872 painting *After the Duel*, by the Italian painter Antonio Mancini: a boy dressed all in black as if in mourning, against an ochre wall, in the foreground a blood-splattered white shirt. Was the boy the assassin, was the deceased an enemy, a brother, a father, a lover, all of these? "The painting didn't reveal the story behind its subject, and so remained an enigma, which I always like." I look at the painting now online, the tiled multiplicity of the boy's pasty delicate profile in the resulting image search. The delicacy too of his lace collar. How his curly head is thrown back, against the wall. There is something unreadable in his expression. Is it forlorn, or bratty and defiant, or perhaps numbed? It is such a morbid yet voluptuous portrait, a miniature of what Guibert's work is for me. Guibert searches everywhere for facts of the Italian painter's life—when he was 20 he painted this boy, named Luigello, many times over, as a street acrobat, as a thief, an obsessive desire for his muse that mirrors Guibert writing in earlier years of his all-encompassing passion for the teenage Vincent, like his own drug, like all the drugs consumed in the work. Mancini knew Manet and Degas in Paris. Later he was involuntarily committed by his family in a psychiatric hospital, when he returned to society he began to paint conventional portraits of the bourgeoisie instead of homoerotic dreamscapes. He was buried with his paintbrush and the *Manual* of Epictetus, which, Guibert writes to us, follows Marcus Aurelius's *Meditations* in the yellow Garnier-Flammarion editions Muzil gives to him from his library months before his death.

I had planned to take the train this summer to Philadelphia to see the Mancini collection there for the Guibert study—it never happened. Like really my Guibert pilgrimage in Paris, although I did make it to the Manet room at the Musée d'Orsay, where I was also there to view an exhibition of Paula Rego paintings, for a catalogue essay I had promised to write. We couldn't get the travel stroller up and down any of the stone stairs, my child cranky and wanting to trek back across the Tuileries to the carousel, where we paid for her to go round and round clinging to the ostrich, which resembled one of Rego's dancing studies in black tulle, her weird amalgam of Disney and Degas. I had little time to stroll around the Tuileries and think of the flânerie of Baudelaire and Manet. I did quickly snap photographs on my phone of *The Balcony*, which I allowed myself to at least stop and consider. I've always been intrigued by the framing of the strange green shutters, the shadow obscuring what is inside the room, made even more eerie by the darkness in the gallery. Manet's canvas like a window, according to Foucault in a 1971 lecture given in Tunisia. "And all of this great hollow space, this great empty space which normally must open onto a depth, why is it rendered invisible to us and why does it render us invisible?" The morbidity and disconnection of the three figures, how strange and skewed they sit in that space, between light and dark, inside and outside. What is waxen Berthe Morisot, with her fan and dark curls, gazing at? It strikes me that the qualities Foucault writes about in Manet's paintings could also describe Guibert's writing—the textures of density and lightness, how his paragraphs feel like objects.

The role of the reader is to look through these windows, but there is a shadow obscuring what is inside.

The balcony from which Guibert's narrator remembers gazing across at his famous neighbor, before they were to become intimates, watching him exit in that black leather jacket with chains. For my trip to Paris, I had ambitiously researched a list of Guibert-related addresses to visit, almost none of which I made it to, except for the hospital where Foucault died and the Manet room. I never saw the wax heads at Musée Grévin and the cabinets of curiosities at the Musée de l'Homme—objects of his photographic obsession. While in Paris, Hedi wrote me that Foucault's apartment was at 285 rue de Vaugirard, so I knew Guibert's apartment was nearby. In our hotel bed at night, my daughter watching *Wizard of Oz* on the iPad, I read on Google Books in a book of criticism that it was a sixth-floor walk-up at 293 on the same street, two doors down. (In the novel he gives his address instead at 203 rue du Bac, a slipperiness that occurs throughout, playing subtly with the facts of his life.) Guibert's real-life apartment was now above a grocery store. Between the two apartments was a Lebanese restaurant. But where it was, in a nondescript area in the fifteenth arrondissement on the Left Bank, was far away from the Canal Saint Martin area where we were staying, and from anywhere else we wanted to go, and it was difficult getting anywhere in Paris with a child. We took Ubers everywhere, holding our daughter on our lap, even though we never used rideshares at home.

While attempting to excavate the surface of my desk this spring, I find the postcard from a couple years ago that Sofia sent to me from Paris, before my trip there. In the postcard Sofia notes that she is currently reading a biography of Rilke, as she and her family were next visiting the Duino Castle, thinking towards one of her infinite research projects. I'm realizing, she writes me, I am less interested in reading the lives of these writers, it's all about when they die. I am still alive! she ends the postcard, which she knows I will recognize as one of On Kawara's conceptual projects, where he sent almost 900 telegrams to various friends and acquaintances in the art world, with various minimal, comic texts: I AM STILL ALIVE, I AM NOT GOING TO COMMIT SUICIDE DON'T WORRY, I AM NOT GOING TO COMMIT SUICIDE WORRY, and my personal favorite, I AM GOING TO SLEEP FORGET IT.

Because Sofia and I have become accustomed to quoting, sometimes without citation, each other's letters in our recent work, I often also think of the slipperiness of how Sebald writes friendship—the friends whose words or life the narrator appropriates in writing without the use of quotations, instead interjecting the occasional "he said" in the mode of Thomas Bernhard. It has become a shorthand for us to speak of the chapter in *Rings of Saturn* documenting a visit to the Suffolk home of his friend Michael Hamburger. Beyond appearing as a character in the novel, Hamburger also was the English translator of Sebald's poetry. Sofia and I also often discuss how translation is also a form of writing, or rewriting—an uncanniness of voice, a ventriloquism. When the Sebald narrator first looks at Michael Hamburger's desk, "a strange feeling came upon me," that what he is seeing is actually his own abandoned, heavy mahogany desk, no longer worked at because the room was too cold. This scene is illustrated with a photograph of a wooden desk covered with papers in front of a window, the grids recalling the opening passage, when the narrator remembers convalescing in a hospital room and dragging himself to the window to look outside, pulling

himself up, remembering that gesture of Gregor Samsa trem-
blingly climbing a chair and looking outside, forgetting the
feeling of freedom a window once afforded. The contrast of
the more open grid of the desk window versus the tighter black
netting of the hospital window at the beginning.

The photograph in *Rings of Saturn* of what we assume to be
Michael Hamburger's unoccupied desk piled with papers in front
of an open window also resembles one of Guibert's unpeopled
photographs of his desk or bookshelf that stands in for the self
otherwise absent, except as a shadow or in the stilled camera's
gaze. There are also the interiors Guibert took of himself among
the various writing materials and assemblages on his desk, like
Sienne, 1979, a young muscular body bent over his desk in front
of the window, smoke curling upwards like a halo, as if suggesting
some block or doom. Although Guibert appeared to rarely experience writer's block, except for the days when his body was stopped
by illness. Not the same late-middle-age dusty gloom that Sebald
and Hamburger shared from their respective perches in Suffolk and Norfolk, like Sofia and I, who often write to each other
about having no will or inclination to write, or perhaps we mean
space and time. The moment in *Rings of Saturn* when the Sebald
narrator's exhaustion over the futility of literary work blends with
his friend's, it is difficult to tell who is speaking or thinking:

> For days and weeks on end one racks one's brain to no avail,
> and if asked, one could not say whether one goes on writing
> purely out of habit, or a craving for admiration, or because one
> knows not how to do anything other, or out of sheer wonder-
> ment, despair, or outrage, any more than one could say whether
> writing renders one more perceptive or more insane. Perhaps
> we all lose our sense of reality to the precise degree to which we

are engrossed in our own work, and perhaps that is why we see in the increasing complexity of our mental constructs a means for greater understanding, even while intuitively we know that we shall never be able to fathom the imponderables that govern our course through life.

Instead in the black-and-white photographs of Guibert's desk, often titled simply *Table de travail*, or worktable, there is a sense of peaceful industriousness and contemplation that recalls the light and organization of St. Jerome's studioli as rendered by Albrecht Dürer. The beautiful piles of little notebooks against the pages of manuscript, all rendered with Guibert's orderly handwriting, next to his typewriter. Even the nighttime gloominess of his small desk at the Villa de Médicis, taken in 1988, the year he was diagnosed, has a goth feeling of a vanitas still life, the desk with its blackened flower arrangement, the piles of manuscript pages, always a miniature frame of a Renaissance portrait, set amidst a massive backdrop of translucent curtains. Another more chaotic *table de travail* is still a staged mise en scène showing work, which is showing time, presumably late at night—a champagne bottle and glass, Old Masters postcards, photographs of friends, always the rotary telephone, papers stacked throughout. For the past year my desk sat mostly unused in the nursery, only liminally still my office, covered with piles of papers and notebooks relating to the Guibert study that I have been attempting these past three years. For some time my out-of-print red-and-blue Serpent's Tail edition of *To the Friend* lay in a dust pile behind the door, next to a small yellow plastic Play-Doh container, a tiny white sock, and a collection of Bolaño nonfiction.

Today is the first time in months I've sat at the desk, moved from the former office, presently the child's room, into the living room. Now my desk sits in front of an open window with veiled curtains like the ones Guibert would photograph like shrouds or bridal veils, suggestive of the sacraments (including the witty *Le fiancé*, featuring Thierry). There is a large hole in one of the cheap gauzy curtains framing the front window, as my dog Genet has torn it while barking psychotically at postal workers. Often I work instead on the couch, covered with notebooks and books, laptop positioned precariously. I identify with the portrait of the Flaubert scholar at the beginning of *Rings of Saturn*, whose archives have closed in on her to the point that she sits on a chair, scribbling, but being able to point to the pertinent folder or file, reminding the Sebald narrator of Dürer's angel of melancholy.

In *To the Friend*, four months after Muzil's death, the narrator is asked by Stéphane, Muzil's companion, to photograph his apartment as it was left, partially for legal reasons, but also for the future archive. The thread of tension throughout, the ways those around him wanted to protect how the philosopher would be remembered. It is the first time that the narrator has set foot in the apartment he so often frequented since his friend's death, where everything is covered with dust in his absence, as if under a deep sleep. "The day was overcast, but light broke miraculously through the clouds when I got out my camera." He uses his small Rollei 35 for the artwork in the living room, the drawing by Picabia, and the African masks. He borrowed Jules's Leica for the up-close photographs, like an artfully composed image of the wastebasket holding a crumpled envelope with an unfinished address in Muzil's handwriting, a classic Guibert framing, both domestic and melancholy. In the cupboards stacks of manuscripts instead of glasses or dishes, "the outlines and rough drafts of the endless book, which had escaped destruction," unlike the other manuscripts Muzil destroyed, denying a necessary source of potential income for Stéphane, a fact which he is yet to discover. On the sofa piles of material for an essay that was never written, because of time, and also because Muzil's mind had already begun to deteriorate. In counterpoint to this bookish chaos, he snaps a single photograph of Muzil's spartan windowless bedroom with the mattress on the floor, reminiscent of the monkish way that Wittgenstein lived. The narrator had never before seen that room that Muzil had kept private, but Stéphane wished for a photograph of the bed. He snaps the photograph, although he has run out of film, so the image of the spare unoccupied bed on the floor becomes what Guibert calls in his collection on photography a ghost image, along with all the other photographs that were never printed, the negatives simply handed over for documentation. In revisiting this space and taking these photographs, Guibert describes being freed from a haunting "by drawing a circle around the ruined stage where my friendship had been played out," perhaps, to be able to write about this friendship in the novel. One of my favorite Guibert photographs, which I first saw in an exhibition downtown curated by Moyra Davey and Jason Simon many years ago, is of the shadow of the photographer looming over a bleached white couch or bed, scattered with letters, the title tells us, from Mathieu. Something of that photograph reminded me of what I wanted to write about.

My daughter climbs up on my lap, wanting to know if I am drawing in my notebook. I explain to her that I am writing by hand. Well, writing is like drawing, she says, thoughtfully. She wants to mimic my squiggles with my pen. We practice writing her name together. My notes all filled with her name in uneven capital letters. As opposed to painting, Guibert begins drawing simple objects, like bottles of ink, then later waxen ex-votos of children from his trip to Lisbon, not yet ready to draw living faces, or his own, which he anticipates as a death mask. There is also something of the energy of drawing throughout the novel. Like a series of sketches—quick, immediate, intimate, nothing so deadly as a more formal and final work. As happens each time I finish a book, after having it out in the world, I am unsure if I'm a writer anymore. I desire to go back into a space where writing feels private. Working on this feels like knitting, like what drawing was for Guibert (or also what drawing is for Renee Gladman in her *Calamities*). Perhaps, Sofia writes me, this is the real space of writing, the space of not-writing. She writes me, Your knitting comparison reminds me of Flaubert: "I have condemned myself to write for myself alone, for my own personal amusement, the way one smokes or rides." John reads this passage. He thinks I should take out this bit about knitting. Do you even know how to knit? he asks me, knowing that I find anything that resembles craft boring, that I lack the talent or manual dexterity or at least the desire for those sorts of time-intensive hobbies, although certainly I would benefit from having something else to occupy me. He's the one that sews patches when needed, using his knowledge of binding books. Let's work on your fine motor function, I say to my child, encouraging her to thread or stack or cut something with scissors. But Guibert uses this knitting analogy as well. "I haven't done a stitch of work on this book in the last few days," he says at one point in the novel. It's become almost banal, to link textiles with writing—to weave, to knit, to thread. But there's something to this in terms of how I work out writing—to knit together, to sometimes tear apart at the seams. Writing for me has that tactile function—it not only fills the time, it is time for me. I was taught to knit as a young girl, I say to John. I was taught all of those feminine crafts—crocheting, sewing, knitting. I had one of those boards where I was supposed to needlepoint little pictures. My sister and I would sit with the female elders, while they also knitted or needlepointed, as a sports game droned in the background that the men and boys watched. I still remember, sitting with my cousin on a couch at my grandmother's, as she taught me how to braid my doll's hair, and then later, how to knit a simple scarf, with my own set of child's needles, working on a row at a time, tearing it out when I got it wrong. I remember something of the manual rhythm of the looping and wrapping. The sharpness of the needles. The spongey ball of yarn. She was always so joyous, my cousin, an excellent cook and baker. A pity she wasn't allowed to finish high school, she had to take care of her sick mother. She never married . . . my cousin who lived with a taciturn butch woman we also called cousin, whom she met while working at the Motorola factory. She died atrociously of liver disease, in poverty, having to quit her job as a grocery cashier once she got sick. Not long after her partner died of lung cancer, around the same time my mother died of the same disease. The carefully put together scrapbooks at my cousin's wake, she was in a group with my mother . . . Something catches in my throat as I write this, I've already written this before, how did I get here, caught up in my childhood memories . . .

Can I focus back on the problem I've been thinking through for years, the problem enacted by a friendship? Copied into my notes from Gide's journal: "Each book up to now has been the exploitation of an uncertainty."

I "met" my friend now a decade ago in the chaotic and open space of literary blogs, a space that has now almost totally disappeared, or become more corporate and professionalized, or migrated and morphed elsewhere. At the time I was living in a small town in the middle of the country, a town where I knew no one save for my partner, who was at work all day in the library of the state university. One day, an email with an unfamiliar address showed up in my inbox, a response to a post I had written about Fernando Pessoa's heteronyms. Let me introduce myself, the letter began. I am a writer who blogs and comments on a handful of other blogs under another name in order to attempt to have *sincere, authentic* conversations about literature. The author of the letter, who had been commenting on my blog under the name of Alex Suzuki, felt certain that I had guessed her secret, which was that she had been responding to my blog, and a handful of other kindred blogs and online diaries, under this pseudonym, or more accurately, this heteronym, like Pessoa's, as her alter ego had a slightly different ethnic makeup, age, gender presentation, even, it turned out, a different voice and writing style. I recognized the name as appearing fairly regularly in the comment box, as well as the cerebral yet chatty quality of the voice. Part of me found these original comments annoying in the way they seemed to argue my same points more succinctly, or maybe just the general irritation I can feel at others' eloquence, but I remember feeling pleased by her engagement as well. This was someone, I remember thinking at the time, who had read a lot of critical theory, judging from the way jargon sometimes cluttered her language. It can feel like remembering a stranger, recalling the indistinct first encounters with a soon-to-be intimate, although an intimate on the internet whom I had never met and only wrote to, so an encounter entirely with language.

I remember that the letter came as both a surprise to me and also no surprise at all—it made sense that none of us, I mean the handful of writers who regularly commented on one another's blogs, were who we said we were online, and that the names that we gave were often only covers or aliases for the multiplicity of identities we wished to explore in writing in this way.

I wonder at these opposing desires in us as writers—the simultaneous desire to disappear and to be known. I think I might understand this more now than I did then. For I didn't write a blog under a pseudonym—but perhaps, again, pseudonym is not the right term either, for pseudonym means false name and this is not accurate in the case of Alex Suzuki, Alex Suzuki was a fiction rather than false, and there can perhaps be more truth in a fictitious identity than in one's public persona, which is often assumed to stand in for one's authentic self. In his essay "Identity without the Person," Giorgio Agamben traces back "persona" to the theater of the Stoics, the actor depicted holding the mask at a distance, a gap between the self and persona that Western concepts of identity has obliterated—point to the mask. In this *professional mode of being*, Alex Suzuki wrote to me, in this initial letter, with the new and bewildering world of status and hierarchies and appearances and names, is there any room for actual conversation? Under the polished veneer of reputation, is there any space left for the real? Blogging was like being a writer and a reader at the same time, she went on to write, being able to interact directly and personally with the writer, an intimate experience that spoke to what literature should be at its core. Perhaps, she wrote me, her alter ego was more real—more authentic at least—than the name by which she was known. If she blogged under her professional name, it would possibly help her career, but for her it would also destroy her soul in the process. It would feel inauthentic to her, and thus inauthentic to the *project of literature*. She knew this because she once had a blog where she would weigh in on the various debates in the poetry world under her "real" name, as well as on the poetry listservs from before my time. There are others, perhaps, who can successfully blend their personal and their public selves, or *author-function*, a term of Foucault's she would frequently utilize, blending these two in a kind of public writing that feels authentic to themselves, but she was not one of them, she wrote. My blog, she thought, was one example of such blending. There was much more to what she wrote, and more eloquently than I can reproduce here. She apologized then for this long confession. Doesn't the very act of becoming an author amount to the creation of a public persona apart from one's personal self? And yet literature itself is where the truest things can be said. Fiction of fictions! she ended the letter. We live in paradox.

I realized at the time that this initial salvo was a test to see who in what she called the *professional literary world* would respond to a nobody, albeit a brilliant one. This was not a challenge for me as I was a nobody as well, and grateful to converse with anyone about writing. Apparently I passed, as we began communicating in the comments and often on the same Gmail thread throughout the day, on topics dominated by what I was sketching out at the time, some aspects of which were so puerile on my part that I think about these posts, and the book that was to follow, with some embarrassment, although also admiration for how intense and earnest I was at the time. I also feel embarrassment now for how speedy my correspondence was with Alex Suzuki, how green and unthought out my replies, an embarrassment powerful enough that it's difficult to actually look at the correspondence, so it exists as a ghost, even as I write this. I used to think writing should come out with the speed of thought, but lately I long more towards slowness.

There was a different intimacy to our communication then than the emails I get about once a week now, sent to one of my teaching email addresses, the one that is publicly available online. When readers write me now, I feel like I shouldn't be included in the conversation. I am no longer the person who wrote that book, who wrote any of the books, and am not sure I can speak for them, although that is the expectation. Just this week an exchange with a doctoral student at Oxford who wanted to ask about the role of the fictional narrator in one of my early novels. She wanted to know what I thought about Roland Barthes's death of the author, about the writer and reader dynamic, about fixed meaning. It was a heady series of existential questions that I mostly didn't have an answer for. I don't think the narrator is the author, I wrote to her. I don't think I am the narrator. Although sometimes I'm not sure if I'm the author anymore either. After I publish a book I am so emptied out of it, outside of it, I am not sure I even can comment on it. I am not sure who "I" am really. The work becomes the reader's to write into—I'm not sure it has anything to do with me anymore.

At the opening of my correspondence with Alex Suzuki I would repeatedly inquire as to the contours and direction of her project of anonymity, of where it was going to go, as if it had to go somewhere. She told me she was inspired in part by the practice of Chinese artists conducting their careers under a pseudonym, although it's not exactly the same, she noted, as the real identities of these artistic pseudonyms are usually common knowledge, whereas she invented Alex Suzuki in order to kill off her *public author persona*. She both is and is not Alex Suzuki, she wrote me, and she wanted Alex Suzuki to have an autonomous existence, which is why she has her own Blogger, Gmail, and Goodreads accounts. She had this even down to her alter ego's middle name, which curiously was the same as mine, Marie, in her full-name Gmail address. The pseudonym is not a form of hiding, she wrote to me, it's about a utopian concept of literature, recalling what Foucault said in an interview, that all authors should conduct a one-year experiment where they publish without names. I find the passage in a collection of his posthumously published interviews titled *Foucault Live* in an early Semiotext(e) edition, with a black and white photograph of the back of his bald head filling the back cover:

> I will propose a game: *the year without names*. For one year books will be published without the author's name. The critics will have to manage with an entirely anonymous production. But I suspect that perhaps they will have nothing to say: all the authors will wait until the next years to publish their books.

I love that little dig at the end, that authors, despite their longing towards disappearance, would not actually consent to publish anonymously. In Guibert's novel, we are told "Muzil had become obsessed with his own name. He wanted to obliterate it." The narrator suggests that he submit a piece for the newspaper under a pseudonym. He is delighted in his invention of Julien d'Hôpital. "What flash of insight told you that the problem isn't the head, but the name?" Of course the editors refused to publish it, because they wanted a piece from Foucault, or Muzil. I too commissioned an essay from Alex Suzuki, for the online journal I was asked to guest-edit, surreptitiously being instructed to invite only women writers to contribute by the male editor, which in retrospect felt like a stunt. I am not sure I identify any more as a woman writer, she wrote to me when I asked her to submit work under Alex Suzuki. At the time I didn't understand it but now I do, even often have felt this way myself. But I wonder now whether this has evolved for her. Later, she clarified, she considered her alter ego, her Alex, to be more of a woman writer, and more of an essayist, less of a fiction writer. She submitted a poetic essay from the point of view of an extra in a studio film from

Hollywood's Golden Age, a hovering supernumerary. I remember a line from it well: "Invisible in my visibility, I stare out from the screen with the equanimity of a nobody."

I was at that point in my writing life where I thought every impulse had to be distilled into a "project," as opposed to embracing the ephemeral, as Alex Suzuki had. I was so fascinated by her heteronym experiment, which I tried to contextualize within performance art, projects often without an object, marked by neither reproduction nor formal documentation. I'll have to think about your concept of writing as performance art, she wrote to me during one such volley. If what I'm doing is a form of performance, she picked up this thread sometime later, it's not relational, like Marina Abramovic and Ulay walking the Great Wall to meet each other and then go their separate ways, but more solitary. She had just been studying the catalogue of Tehching Hsieh's one-year performances, which took place almost entirely in isolation. Perhaps something of his ethos speaks to the solitary aspect of writerly performance, she wrote to me. The Tribeca loft cage he lived in for 365 days for his 1978–1979 Cage Piece. The time clock he punched every hour from 1980–1981. The subsequent year he spent entirely outside. The year he spent tied by a rope to Linda Montano. The one year he promised, from 1985–1986, not to make any art (No Art Piece). His rules he set forth for his final Thirteen Year Plan, from 1986–1999, where he promised to make art but not show it publicly. In a recent interview with *The Believer*, the artist spoke about one of the art pieces he made during that time, which he entitled *Disappearance*, which began in 1991, where he tried to leave society, journeying to Alaska but only ending up as far as Washington State. He found it impossible to leave society, but still he was a stranger, which reminded him of the isolation he felt when he first arrived in this country in 1974 from Taiwan, an exile which catalyzed his original performances. He only was able to continue the project for half a year. In 2000, he emerged from solitude with the note: "I kept myself alive." I glean from the interview that he now owns a dumpling shop in Brooklyn near where my daughter used to go to preschool, when the schools were open. I'm not sure if he is still making art, although there is something process-oriented and time-based about making dumplings, which are certainly more practical objects than performances or books, so there is a logic to his career change, one more pragmatically grounded in sustenance and living. But perhaps this too will be claimed at some point as a project.

I came to realize that rather than existing in the *professional literary world*, the alter-Alex Suzuki was a specific name in what she also referred to as the *poetics coterie*, more specifically a group of experimental prose writers writing after or in the late phase of the 1990s literary movement of New Narrative, based partly in the Bay Area. Her first and, at the time, only book, became a minor classic of the movement, while not a commercial success, for surely it only sold a few hundred copies. Early in our correspondence, in the intensity of our back and forth, much of it while she was at her full-time job, Alex Suzuki accidentally wrote me back via her real-name email address. In my reply I pretended it didn't happen, until she realized what she had done. So the coming out process, as it feels appropriate to call it, was in two parts: first Alex Suzuki came out to me as a pseudonym or heteronym, and then she came out to me as the name she was known by in real life, meaning with her wife, her job, and among the poets, her real or given name. I began to think of Alex Suzuki and the other-Alex Suzuki as separate entities, bearing different personality traits, advice strategies, even writing styles, a distinction which Alex Suzuki actually created herself by speaking of the

alter-Alex Suzuki as well as Alex Suzuki in the third person. Alex
Suzuki was Japanese, an office temp, and several years younger
than her other self, who was of Chinese descent and worked
in middle-management in Silicon Valley. I'm unsure of Alex
Suzuki's sexuality, though alter-Alex Suzuki was in a committed
relationship with another woman, albeit with a partner who did
not know about her online writing experiment, although she was
otherwise a close participant in her partner's writing life, serving
as her editor over the years and years it took for her to work on
each book in progress.

Recently I reread her first novel, a *bildungsroman* written from the
point of view of a "we," which documents a longing for community and a failure of a "we," finding alienation and absurdity—for
she was often very funny—in the concept of an "I." I was surprised
to find therein a meditation on tone. I've been trying to think
about tone in writing as spatial—the idea that language as we
encounter it on the page can take up space within us like a room.
That tone is something like a feeling or frequency. And I realize that I really fell in love with the exuberance of Alex Suzuki's
writing voice, which always felt conspiratorial, first in the space
of the comment box, then in the ongoing thread of email. At
the time I was also reading and rereading *To the Friend Who Did
Not Save My Life*, falling in love with the way Guibert's gossipy
and also exuberant tone took up the space of each page, the way
the pages of his book were like boxes too—boxes or windows
or photographs. In our ongoing correspondence we collectively
drafted our theory of emotions. In her superlative way she began
to write me, still obliquely, of the *great coronary heartbreak* she
experienced when ostracized years back from her writing community, with whom I had corresponded in my brief tenure volun-
teering with a small press that often republished the orphan texts

of New Narrative, and also during my even briefer participation in an avant-garde feminist collective. All of these poets my friend had known in a previous life, a community of brilliant but difficult, in both meanings of the word, minor writers, who like Alex Suzuki wrote a poet's novel every decade or so. Perhaps community is not the best word for it, this loose grouping of writers for whom writerly ambition and commerce were viewed with suspicion. During our correspondence I would vent to her about my interactions with these various poets in my role at a small press, how I unknowingly caused tensions by agreeing to read so-and-so's manuscript, not fully grasping the power dynamics of who published or rejected whom, who was partnered up with whom, both now and in the past, not fully grasping the shifting undercurrents resulting in cold shoulders and the exiting of rooms at literary conferences. Later I realized that what amounted to gossip, which was my attempt to understand the intricacies of how a writing community worked, caused the opening of old wounds for Alex Suzuki.

In her initial letter, Alex Suzuki wrote to me that she had been reading Claudia Rankine's *Don't Let Me Be Lonely*, a book that was also formative for me, where Rankine quotes Paul Celan comparing a poem to a handshake. A poem is a personal exchange, a meeting and an agreement, a point of contract, and more than anything an act of trust, she wrote me. And she has found that trust is the most difficult thing to sustain in the *professional literary world*, where there is so much competition, careerism, and backstabbing. I know when she wrote me this confession, in this first email, she was asking me not to betray her. I've struggled with this in the years since I've attempted to write about our friendship, in the decade or so I've been haunted by our communication. At what point does the writing become an act of betrayal?

In our correspondence we also referenced *Century of Clouds*, Bruce Boone's New Narrative work that was a friendship, like the original subtitle to Thomas Bernhard's *Wittgenstein's Nephew*, a genre of writing I feel increasingly drawn to. Told with a collective "we," Boone explores the transformative potentials of being together at a Marxist seminar, with among others, Fredric Jameson and Terry Eagleton, including a fight about sexism during a volleyball game. I never read the novel that the writer behind Alex Suzuki worked on during the time we corresponded. I knew that it was about a collaborative experiment, centering upon a team of misfits set in a suburban malaise who set about performing John Cage's 4'3" in various environments across the country, not documenting that they were doing so except through correspondences with each other on online forums. The thesis of the project, I believe, was more or less about art being without an object, the desire to find silence within noise.

That brings me to another of the inspirations for her online experiment, a passage from an interview with Foucault where he said:

> What strikes me is the fact that in our society, art has become something which is related only to objects and not to individuals, or to life. That art is something which is specialized or which is done by experts who are artists. But couldn't everyone's life become a work of art? Why should the lamp or the house be an art object, but not our life?

Alex Suzuki also connected the notebooks we kept online to Foucault's essay on "self writing," which engages with the ancient Greek practice of the *hypomnemata*, a daily regime of writing in a notebook that had to do with working on the self, or *askesis*, as opposed to producing a commodified object. Whenever I kept on pushing her to describe the outlines of her project, she always maintained that for her, Alex Suzuki was her *pure reader-function*, and she wouldn't want her *author-function* to taint that and potentially kill it. Now, as I write this, from the vantage point of having published seven books, a number that feels excessive, and trying to write a study of Hervé Guibert but distracting myself by writing the story of this friendship, I have come to see that it is more important to be a reader than a writer, even though society places more status on writing, on producing consumable objects, than on reading, which is an ephemeral, solitary activity. I don't know why I needed to push Alex Suzuki to publish more work beyond blog posts, comments, and emails, as opposed to seeing, as I do now, the humility of being a reader. Lately I have been able to pick away, when I have an hour or so, at this story, but I have not been able to read, which makes me feel like an egoist—why do I need to take up space, when I just had a book come out—and like a failure as a participant in the greater project of literature. Sometimes it is just too borderless, to be a reader, to fall in love with another voice, as opposed to the hermetic space of writing one's own text, which you are then arrogant to expect others to read. I write this to Sofia, who agrees with me that it's far more of a moral project to be a reader, and not at all to be a writer, or at least an author. How bitter at the world and full of despair I can feel, Sofia writes to me, and how much I realize this can be cured by an hour of reading. She then sends me a quote by Fernando Pessoa: "Seeing is so superior to thinking, and reading is superior to writing! I may be deceived by what I see but at least I never think it's mine. What I read may depress me, but at least I'm not troubled by the thought I wrote it." Ha ha, Sofia writes.

Alex Suzuki was not sure how far Alex Suzuki, the project, would go, Alex Suzuki wrote to me then. Sometimes I think I'm driven to pursue the Alex Suzuki project the way Genet must have been driven to steal, she wrote. Maybe you are like my gallerist signing and verifying the authenticity of my timecards. Although actually I'm realizing that Alex Suzuki is not an art project but a personal, even spiritual project, a project to save alter-Alex's literary soul. There will never be a time when alter-Alex stands up at a conference panel and announces that she invented Alex Suzuki. I feel that Alex Suzuki could write a book, Alex Suzuki wrote to me. I wonder, though, how alter-Alex could handle this, emotionally. Right now Alex Suzuki exists in concentrated bursts of time, in occasional correspondence, blog entries, blog comments. A book would require more commitment, and how would Alex Suzuki do the expected hustle of reading live and promoting a book? Even if Alex winds up publishing book reviews or poems, which could happen, she'll always identify as an outsider writer, she wrote to me, which is also how I identified at the time. I Alex-identify as an unpublished writer, anything but an author.

There's a parallel between how Alex Suzuki identified as an unpublished writer, her efforts to keep this alter ego separate from professional endeavors, and Kafka's desire to not disrupt the privacy of his nocturnal notebooking and writing activities with the judgment of society, including his family. Alex Suzuki's day job writing technical manuals echoes Kafka's own middle management position writing accident reports, both choosing to make a living off writing that was directly opposed to the imaginative spaces of their own creative work. I think to the clinical horror of the line-drawing illustration of cut-off fingers accompanying Kafka's technical essay from 1910, "Six Measures for Preventing Accidents for Wood-Planing Machines." The funny thing is that despite his desire to keep his world separate, Kafka's insurance firm was full of aspiring poets, a reminder that it is fairly commonplace to want to be a writer or poet. It is more unusual to stay a writer despite lack of status or outward success, to sacrifice sanity, sleep, positive well-being, health, to instead dwell in a life that is one of almost constant paranoia, oscillating between horror at invisibility and nausea at visibility.

There is a privilege to being able to cloister oneself off with one's art from commerce, to be able to write one book a decade for a small community of mostly poets. As I write this, I realize that Alex Suzuki most likely made an upper-middle-class salary, with job security, and benefits. She owned a house in the Bay Area when I will likely never transcend being a renter. I too live in an extremely expensive city, albeit paying rent month to month, now with dependents, and often barely scraping by, even though I still spend too much money on clothes. She didn't have to deal with connecting writing to financial pressures. It was easier then, perhaps, for her, to look down upon the idea of making any money at writing, or needing to make money at writing, a position I maintained for years as well, getting barely by with adjunct teaching gigs in cheaper cities, until I didn't have that freedom any longer. I wonder if the decade it would take her to write and intensely revise a slim, perfectly calibrated novel was because of lack of time, due to having a 9 to 5, forcing her writing into the night and weekends, or because she allowed herself to take the time, not having the vulgar necessity of speed. In this current environment of precarity, this so-called gig economy, it is difficult not to romanticize *a job that ends*, just like many romanticize being a writer so as *to not have a job*, to have one's hours to one's self after a certain time, to have weekends, to not have capitalism suck up all available energy and possible time, not having to work constantly, including often for free, in this nebulous and borderless realm of publicizing one's self and one's work, in order to continue, not even to succeed, but just to continue. Although both possibilities are most likely fictions. Maybe the only way to truly luxuriate in thinking and time was to be independently wealthy.

I don't remember exactly why Alex Suzuki immolated her blog, as we were all wont to do temporarily in times of distress or feeling like we had emoted too much online, and as most of us have now done permanently. I recall there were rumors as to her real identity, as her entries began to be more widely circulated and read within our small community, which I might be partially responsible for. She had also come out to a couple of the other bloggers. Jackie Wang, having guessed correctly who she was, asked if I could put her in touch with the reclusive author, an inquiry I meekly forwarded on to Alex Suzuki in an email. The husband of one of us, a poet, began to comment on her blog in such a way that suggested he knew she was an important writer, when he had never commented on any of our blogs before, in that similar way that writers look at you differently at literary conferences once they recognize the name on the nametag, which was of course everything Alex Suzuki hated. At the same time her novel that she had worked on for a decade was finally coming out, and she had to bear, as all published writers do, that curious period of both desiring and sometimes being given brief recognition and visibility and feeling more often than not invisible in the grand scheme of the publishing world.

After we had been out of contact for some time, we made a plan to meet, after I contacted her to let her know I would be giving a reading in her city. I was embarking on a tour of bookstores and conferences for my second novel, which was initially published by a small-press publisher who kept on pitching quixotic corporate marketing strategies, including reading at Sephoras all over the country. (He had also suggested to a distinguished author that she read at Bed Bath & Beyonds, which he saw as her target demographic, where he assumed women of late middle age would congregate.) I financed the tour entirely by myself, as is the expectation, which cost me thousands that I did not have, and I said yes to all and any publicity, as is also the expectation, all in the name of *exposure*, which meant writing enough responses to interviews to total the energy and word count of yet another book, in fact a second book about the first, a transparent boring book, a book that instructed the reader how to think and feel about the other book, but this one was available now, freely, online, negating the need to buy or read the first book at all. With the stress of travel, I found my health disintegrating and was in and out of doctor's offices for my mysterious symptoms of inflammation and fatigue, including constant respiratory infections, digestive issues, and debilitating menstrual cramps that I attempted to treat with regular acupuncture back home, which was now in North Carolina. Previously I entertained the fantasy of us meeting for the first time at the modern art museum, and having it be a charged, even romantic, moment. But now, recalling this, I feel foolish, as we were both in monogamous relationships, and I'm not sure I really had those feelings for her, or was just lonely and bored. I wonder now whether Alex Suzuki would have shown up. Although I was the one who ultimately canceled the trip to San Francisco, in order to have a ruptured endometrial cyst removed. I wonder if the fact that she never told her partner about our correspondence contributed to my confusion at times around how our friendship resembled an emotional affair. It would be stupid of me to say I was infatuated with her, as without meeting her it was impossible to know if there was any real spark or attraction. It is more honest to admit that I was in love with her writing voice and the fact that she was writing these letters only to me, an intimacy that mirrored how I felt when I read Hervé Guibert. Sometimes I would need to masturbate after reading one of her lengthy, erudite missives, perhaps in a way to relieve the intensity of the speed of our correspondence (but after all, who doesn't masturbate on occasion to one's friends?). There was an erotics to my friendship with Alex Suzuki, perhaps a one-sided one. The dynamic was more like a tutelage, even though alter-Alex was no more than five or maybe seven or ten years older than me, a distance from my earlier 30s that felt vast, like I was still a girl and she was almost menopausal. I think to the interview that Foucault gave in 1981 on the Socratic ideal of friendship between two men of different ages, "a relationship that is still formless, which is friendship: that is to say, the sum of everything through which they can give each other pleasure." One of the members of Foucault's inner circle of young men in the late 70s and early 80s was a gorgeously cherubic Hervé Guibert. I am reminded of Edmund White's anecdote in his review of Guibert's illness books in the *London Review of Books*, Foucault's whisper-hiss when White brought Susan Sontag to one of Foucault's dinners, after she had left the room: "*Why did you invite her?*"

Perhaps feeling shut out of the larger literary tradition, I was looking for more formless relationships in the process of trying to form myself as a writer, the "desire-in-uneasiness" of the homosocial that Foucault speaks to in the interview. There was previously the intensity of my friendship with the French translator, who published a notebook work every year and always needed to talk through various crises on the phone, where I was expected to agree with them over this or that small yet upsetting event viewed as a betrayal, and continually affirm their genius, although they never recognized me as a serious writer,

in fact seemed annoyed to remember that I was apparently trying to write as well, annoyed at any other writers within their
community. I remember them saying to me, of a mutual friend,
How could she say she's inspired by Duras? She doesn't even read
Duras in the original French! But part of the joy of being in a
community with Alex Suzuki was that she never talked down
to me, and she always engaged seriously with my inquiries. Perhaps this is why I'm so troubled at the desire I've felt for the past
decade to elegize this friendship in writing, which no doubt she
would find a betrayal. With this other relationship at the time,
I knew that they wanted an adoring reader and helpmate, and
that was not at all what Alex Suzuki desired from me, rather she
seemed to seek only authentic conversation.

I suspect that I became ostracized from these other poets when
I became more public, either because of their jealousies, as writers are seldom happy for the success of others, or because of what
I now see as the obnoxious nature of my constant self-promotion.
I'm unsure if that's the cause behind my eventual alienation from
Alex Suzuki. I do know that our correspondence as to our reading
and thinking was so distinct from the competitive and transac-
tional relationships I had found in the small press world, including with the poets, who regarded my work dubiously since I was
a lowly writer of only essays and novels, and not even the right
type of poet's novel, and subsequently in New York, once I had
moved here. I did find other authentic connections with writers
who kept blogs at the same time, and yet I am not haunted by
them, because I am still in touch with many of them. Whereas at
some point Alex Suzuki disappeared from the internet and from
my life. Although, come to think of it, not being online anymore,
I wonder if for others I might have seem to have disappeared, if
I might actually be their Alex Suzuki.

When I canceled the trip to San Francisco because of my surgery, she sent me a note, wishing me well. In the letter, she apologized for her absence, explaining that her mother had just died. I had no idea that her mother had been sick, or that their relationship had apparently been painful and difficult. She didn't know that my mother had died in my early twenties, although I had been working on a book circling around that event, and the event that was my mother, for many years. I had the feeling, she wrote to me, that we were linked like that, when I stumbled upon your blog. Her father had died as well when she was young, although, she wrote, his was a quick and painless death. It felt strange we knew so little about each other's private lives—I wonder now if we were ever so close after all.

And so began the last, almost courteous, loop of our correspondence, both having disappeared our blogs, where we wrote complaints to each other about what it felt like to have books out. I'm thinking about you, I wrote to her at one point, and I hope you're surviving. I think I understand why you immolated your online identity a while ago, I wrote to her, referring to both disappearances, the disappearance of the blog she wrote under her real name, then later the disappearance of the heteronym project of Alex Suzuki. I'm realizing how fucked up so many writers are I'm meeting, no more fucked up than me, but impossible in some way to form any lasting connections with, I wrote to her. She replied to me empathetically as always, always performing far more emotional labor than I, Isn't it strange how touchy people's egos are in the literary world? Frankly, she wrote to me, I'm more afraid of dealing with the women, the men at least are more open about ambition or more able to accept it in others. Sometimes, she wrote to me, I think the only way to get by in this world is to either a) deal with everybody at a strictly professional distance or

b) pretend (à la Duras) that you are already a dead writer. Later, I wrote her and asked her more about the Duras quote. She'd read it in an epigraph, but couldn't remember the exact source. She paraphrased. Maybe writers should write as if they were already dead.

The decision not to do any readings for the new book was both liberating and nerve-racking, Alex Suzuki wrote to me, this constant feeling that she should be promoting herself, jumping on the buzz of recent publication. But she decided for her life and sanity that this was what was necessary for her. Regardless she had developed the habit of checking her Amazon and Goodreads numbers daily, sometimes many times a day. Out of curiosity, I look at the Amazon rankings of her two books. Her first, more influential novel is ranked somewhere around 2 million. But her second novel lingers around 100,000, which is comparable to how many of my own books are selling, or rather not selling, which by mainstream publishing standards is terrible, but by other metrics is not bad. At the time I asked her if she wanted me to use my newly acquired capital to promote her, perhaps we could do an online interview together, an offer which she of course demurred. What is strange about the email that followed is that it could summarize where I am now, even though I still do interviews and promote myself, but am often too exhausted to do as much as I'm expected, and at least I understand more the existential malady of writing a book and then desiring to disappear from it, wanting and even longing for the work to be taken over by readers, but also wanting to have some control over how readers interpret it. Here's the text of her email as I've copied it into my notes:

> At the same time, I've been feeling a lot of my own insecurities lately, needing constant attention and validation, etc. It got almost unbearable last week, and then this week I managed

to calm myself down with this possibly corny mantra: it's not so much what you get as what you give through your writing. I feel frustrated and inadequate when I think I'm not getting what I expect from the book (attention, sales, readers, influence, etc) but then I think of a few instances where I really feel that I was saying something with the book, something that could in fact reach readers and give them something—and I've gotten a few messages of validation that this message was received—and I actually feel content. Maybe this is the problem of being a public writer, this feeling of nagging discontentment constantly. Sometimes I ask if it really matters all that much how many readers I get. Isn't it more important to have just a small number of readers who actually get what you've written and value it, vs a large slew who are ho hum and don't really get it? Maybe I'm trying to be more buddhist about the whole thing, to see writing too as something impermanent, a transitory impermanent activity, and not just a product that can be rated and evaluated.

I know that Alex Suzuki wrote this email, but it feels like I could have as well, not the I as I was then but the I as I am now. A strange feeling comes over me as I read it.

Sometime later, when I began frequently traveling to New York, both to visit my sister, who had just had a baby, and for publishing events, we did eventually meet in person. The grief and rage I felt then, as now, after seeing what remained of my family, all of us cooped up in an Upper West Side rental with huge glass windows during the hurricane when the baby was born. The writer responsible for Alex Suzuki was in New York, having agreed to a reading at the Poetry Project, and I was doing a reading from my novel at St. Mark's, back when it still existed. I had also flown to

New York in order to tape an interview in the *Bookforum* offices. I was struggling with debilitating shoulder pain, which I was medicating with steroids, so I was feeling both wired and out of it. She immediately clocked me, that I was dressed stylishly, and said something to the effect that she didn't realize that I was a fashion person. It's not actually that I had much style, I had just purchased enough of a uniform to fit in. We sat at a vegan restaurant in the Village that also no longer exists and picked at our salads. In person, neither of us had much to say to the other. There was none of the intimacy that I immediately experienced with others when we first met in person. Perhaps that's the melancholy of this friendship, that it didn't exist once we left the tone or voice of our letters. Since then, I've wondered who really pulled away from whom. I've long wondered what Alex Suzuki thinks of me now, if she thinks of me at all. I've become a minor figure in the *professional literary world*, which in New York still means I am a nobody. "In ten years you will be a mover and shaker in the literary world," she had joked earlier in our correspondence. In retrospect, it feels as if she put a curse on me.

One of her last emails was brief, and I'm not sure if I ever responded. She didn't even sign off. What name would she have used?

Kate,

Lately I've been feeling like a real-life Pessoa heteronym.

I still periodically search for her on the internet. All that remains even of the writer behind Alex Suzuki are a few trace reviews and notices. There is one thumbnail photograph of her, floating amidst a sea of others who share her name who are not my Alex Suzuki, or rather the writer behind Alex Suzuki. In this photo she wears a backpack and stares out at a mountainous landscape. It reminds me of Guibert's description of the freeze-frame of Muzil during an appearance on the talk show *Apostrophes*:

> That was the last tape of Muzil I ever watched, for since then I've refused, from fear of the pain it would cause me, to face any other images of his presence, save those of dreams, and his great shout of laughter, which I've preserved forever in a freeze-frame, delights me still, even though I'm somewhat jealous that laughter so fantastic, so impetuous, so luminous, could have burst forth from Muzil at a time just before our friendship was to begin.

It is not the image of Muzil that the Guibert narrator longs for, but the sound of his surprising bellow of laughter, much as it is not the photograph of Alex Suzuki I think about, but the wit and warmth of her voice. I cannot find this interview that Guibert describes in the novel, it doesn't line up with the times that Foucault appeared on *Apostrophes*, a slipperiness with fact that continues throughout the novels. I watch instead a clip on YouTube of Foucault and Noam Chomsky debating human nature, the concentrated orange of the Tang in the pitcher and glasses on the table. Foucault in his blazer and beige turtleneck, his bald head shiny with exertion, chewing furiously on his fingernails.

Only fragments remain online of Alex Suzuki the project, although of course she wouldn't have wanted to call it that. On her Goodreads account, her avatar is that Polaroid of a horn-rimmed Guy Davenport standing next to his bookshelf, languidly wearing a T-shirt bearing the face of a young Ludwig Wittgenstein, an image distilling my sexuality and possibly also my desired gender. There were 210 books in her library. Her last entry was from a decade ago. She was apparently reading Proust and *A Thousand Plateaus*. Forty reviews, all brief essays with her characteristically generous five stars, which she bequeathed upon many of the poets and prose writers in our blogging community. Scrolling through, I realized of course Alex Suzuki, as her own alter ego, had also reviewed her own first novel (which had 136 ratings and an overall rating of 4.35 stars). It is a delicious piece of performative writing, a review that seems to have been written only for me. She writes with her quintessential absurdity juxtaposed with moral seriousness that it had been a while since she last read this book, and she decided to read it again, for no real reason.

> It's a surprisingly witty book (memoir?), quite wry in fact, at the moment when critical theory and cultural politics collide, and the experiences of the day become unreal, and the person becomes unknown to their own lives. The alienation expressed here feels real to me, however, as well as the pathos underneath the depiction of friendships from another era.

The question mark after "memoir" makes me laugh. Is she lightly satirizing the typical reader response or wondering about the instability of the selves characterized within the work, the distancing through the acts of time and writing? There is that line by Roland Barthes I always think to, the epigraph to his own ludic "memoir?"—"It must all be considered as if spoken by a character in a novel."

Also of interest is her review of Paul Auster's *Leviathan*, which reads as a flash theory of the two forms of gendered anonymity in the novel, both the Unabomber character and the character based on Sophie Calle. Since she was versed in the history of conceptual art, I imagine Alex Suzuki was aware that Calle

got her characteristically mischievous revenge in her photo-
book *Double Game*, in which she takes on Auster's character of
Maria as an alter-ego, critiquing in red ink facts from the novel
that differentiate slightly from her personal history, as well as,
among other endeavors, documenting following the imaginary
chromatic diet dictated by the novel, so in effect becoming the
character created for her by another. I remember now, shortly
after her trip to Paris, Sofia wrote me of the Sophie Calle and
Hervé Guibert books shelved together on the bookshelf of the
Russian puppeteer's apartment she stayed at with her family.
I am reminded of the portrait in Sophie Calle's 2003 photo-
book *Exquisite Pain*, of the older Russian man Anatoli, the
stranger she shares a compartment and meals with on the Trans-
Siberian Railway, where she has been traveling from Moscow,
part of her weeks-long train ride to Japan in 1985, where she will
be for months on a fellowship. I like thinking of a Russian puppeteer living in Paris who organizes their bookshelves according
to gossip and friendships—it's how I would ideally organize my
own, if they weren't strewn everywhere by little hands, as they
are currently. It makes sense that the photographers and writers
were friends, catalyzed by a kindred parasitism, even putting each
other in one another's work. I know that a section of *Exquisite
Pain* functions in many ways as a companion or ghost text to
the portrait of Calle and their friendship published in Guibert's
novel more than a decade earlier, but I don't know how to get
access to it again. I last had borrowed it from inter-library loan,
back when that was possible, and my daughter spilled water on
it, slightly waterlogging it and making the colors bleed, and I had
to profusely apologize to the college librarian and offer to pay
for a replacement although it was now out of print and would
have cost hundreds of dollars, luckily the librarian was understanding and I didn't have to. Finally, Moyra Davey sends me her

copy in the mail just as I'm trying to write this. The volume looks like a small gray prayer book, with red foil on the edges. Each page is marked with a red stamp, counting down the 92 "days to unhappiness" since a break-up with the man who was supposed to join Calle in Japan. In chapter 42 of *To the Friend*, Guibert sends up their competitive friendship in his depiction of Anna, who wars with him after he loses a photograph of her as a child taken by her father, which she had lent him to illustrate a profile he wrote of her for *Le Monde*, an episode that culminates in his slamming the door in her face when she goes to his apartment looking for it before her trip. He meets up with "our adventuress" again unexpectedly at the lobby of the Imperial Hotel in Japan (unnamed in Guibert's book), and decides to ignore her, finding her annoying, although she forms part of their travel group, and then later, their friendship is cemented when they visit two Japanese temples. There is a funny-strange scene of visiting a temple at Asakusa with both of them first mistaking a tree punctured by slips of paper bearing unfavorable prophecies as cherry blossoms in bloom. Then later, in Kyoto, it takes them both hours to write the characters in calligraphy of a prayer or wish, while their two other companions are left bored by the slow and painstaking ritual they are both taking such pleasure in. We get Guibert's version of these events in writing, and then in the extended portrait of these days in *Exquisite Pain*, a rewriting back, with accompanying black-and-white photographs, including two striking photographs of Guibert, as well as the tree bearing the weight of the unfortunate divinations. I place both books next to each other on my pillow, which I then photograph with my phone. Many of the texts in *Exquisite Pain* begin, "My love," as letters to her now ex-lover. "My love," begins the opening marking "63 Days to Unhappiness," "You remember Hervé Guibert?" then unfolding her version of events dealing with the photograph, with the recto taken up entirely by Sophie Calle at an unsmiling 7 years old, relaying more or less the same version of events in his novel, except his indifference as to her agitation that the photograph was lost is filtered through her point of view. In both versions, it is clear that they are an odd couple but also twins—she is the conceptual artist prone to a puckish chaos and boundary crossing and he is the more withholding one, although both prone to tempers. It is telling how she characterizes the cat-and-mouse or conceptual nature of their relationship, that when he interviews her for *Le Monde*, he asks her to tell her life story, beginning with the day she was born, which she does, for hours, which feels like something she would do. "So I decided to play the game," she tells us in *Exquisite Pain*. She ends the page when the photograph is returned, "I realized there and then he would make me pay for it." What follows is a photograph of the first two pages of chapter 42 of *To the Friend*. In doing this, Calle not only collapses the boundaries of fiction and nonfiction but also initiates her practice of commenting upon and critiquing, even delighting in, her fictional incarnations, which she would continue with Auster's novel. There is one more scene that's omitted from Guibert's novel, involving them bathing in each other's tubs in their hotel room in Kyoto, and his fury at her violating his privacy again, by opening the door when he is bathing, as she wanted to see him naked, illustrated with a photograph of the empty wooden bath tub. Flipping through the rest of the book, where at one point she follows after a young married couple on the street, just for the pleasure of it, as a way to pass time, just to remember the gesture of following, a miniature of the follow piece that she enacted years earlier in the projects that would become the photobooks *Address Book* and *Suite Vénitienne*, both playful acts of investigation and revenge against men, much like one could interpret both the Anatoli and the Guibert passages in *Exquisite Pain*. The follow piece in miniature at the end of *To the Friend* feels in some ways an homage to Calle, where the narrator keeps running into the pick-up artist Ranieri, who he first sees at the clinic where he's getting his regular bloodwork, through the streets of Rome.

On YouTube, I also watch the film comprised of the video diaries that Sophie Calle made with her estranged lover Greg Shephard during their cross-country trip in his old Cadillac to California in January 1992, them barely speaking to each other, called alternatively *No Sex Last Night* or *Double-Blind.* Although the film is mostly fraught with the melancholic dissolution of another romantic relationship, it also works as an elegy to her friend, with a title card dedicated to Guibert, who died in Paris seven days before the trip. It begins with a voiceover in Calle's heavily accented English, who confesses that part of the catalyst for the trip was not to be in Paris when Guibert died. "Even if this will be a disaster, we will go. At least far enough to symbolically bury my friend Hervé by the sea. I didn't want to wait in Paris for him to die." She tells us that her friend died while she was on the plane to New York to meet Shephard. A sequence of stills of Sophie Calle walking to a dock, and throwing flowers into the ocean, a symbolic gesture that echoes her friends scattering Guibert's ashes off the coast of Elba at around the same time. The voiceover turns to French. I read the translated subtitles, the stills proceeding slowly, as if trancelike.

> Am I too late? Have they already buried you? Yesterday during the wake I felt so isolated, so cut off from you in New York, that I called your machine, just to hear your voice once more.

We hear the beep of an answering machine, and a voice, Guibert's, instructing to leave a message. The Calle narrator doesn't want to hang up on her dead friend, so she leaves a message, which is characteristically funny, sad, and strange at the same time. Do you remember, she said, that time we were in Kyoto, and you took a bath in my water?

The word "disaster" reminds me of Blanchot's book, *The Writing of the Disaster*, which Amazon tells me I purchased at the beginning of the New Year, in 2015, which is around the time I began to attempt to write through my friendship with Alex Suzuki. I am embarrassed that was during a time I still occasionally purchased books on Amazon, but I'm not going to pretend I didn't. I don't have the book in front of me, it's on the shelf in the next room, but I remember being struck by how Blanchot was influenced by his friendships, specifically with Georges Bataille and Emmanuel Levinas. I remember writing in a notebook a line from Blanchot from this book, something like (although this might not be an exact quote): "Friendship is the truth of this disaster." I think Blanchot was trying to say that community was both possible and impossible at the same time. Alex Suzuki would often reference Blanchot to me, that she was longing for a community, in the Blanchot sense, and that she felt, at least temporally, that she had found this community, with me and with others, online. I think this was also true for me.

Recently I was looking at the second novel that Alex Suzuki sent me, a novel I am ashamed to say I still have never read. A postcard fell out, marked by a brief handwritten note. It feels strange to realize that I had never seen her handwriting before. But whose handwriting, after all, was it? It was a Sol LeWitt postcard, one of his instruction drawings for others to realize: "Wall Drawing #46: Vertical lines, not straight, not touching, uniformly dispersed with maximum density, covering the entire surface of the wall." He created it in Paris days after his friend, the artist Eva Hesse, died of a brain tumor in New York City at the age of 34, possibly due to exposure from the polyester resin and fiberglass that she used for her sculptures, although it's difficult to know whether this is myth-making—an artist killed by fealty to her materials. It was his first time making a work with "not straight" lines, inspired by Hesse's own organic and biomorphic forms. Her 1966 piece *Hang Up* was partially fabricated by her friend LeWitt, a sculptural send-up of a painting, a wood stretcher wrapped with bed sheets, a long metal wire extending out from it into the space of the viewer onto the floor in front of the frame. How Hesse felt that this was the first piece that reached the "absurdity or extreme feeling" that she desired in art. I think about how friendship can affect the limits of one's own thinking, how my friend, who was still my friend, most likely was reaching for a similar level of absurdity and feeling in her own life and work. I spend some time thinking about this before I have to go wake my child up from her nap.

II

To Write As If Already Dead

"Studies are often more beautiful than laboured final versions."

—Hervé Guibert, *Compassion Protocol*

YESTERDAY

I felt ready to begin this study *yesterday* when I realized that it was the anniversary of Hervé Guibert's death, December 27, 1991. It was twenty-eight years later to the day. Something of that coincidence made me feel if not ready, then willing to begin this study I have failed to write, or at least to finish, over the past three years. I wanted to formally begin this book *yesterday*, retracing the beginning pages of *To the Friend Who Did Not Save My Life*, the book by Hervé Guibert I have been contracted to write a study about, but this feeling surged inside of me and then faded, and I succumbed again to the couch, my current resting place. The day passed without me being able to write, except for a note marking this coincidence.

Yesterday felt like the first real day of this sickness, I remember it now from before, the taste of death in my mouth. Food smells and tastes too much and also not enough like food, that hard-boiled egg I just attempted felt and tasted like plastic. The coffee, which I'm not supposed to drink in any quantity that would actually activate something, is like hot, slightly acrid brown water. It was just the other day that I craved food from my childhood, that brief window of everything tasting wonderful, on Christmas Day I wanted crudités arranged with ranch dressing on a plate, just like at my grandmother's for the holidays, or the specific way I envisioned half of a red tomato with a full scoop of mayonnaisey tuna inside, even tracing the shape of it in my notebook. Perhaps I can write like this in the morning, when I force myself to sit upright at a desk, with the light coming in.

ONE

I keep opening up to the first numbered page—1—the pronouncement of a first person that is mordant, morbid, teetering on the edge, either of breakdown or revelation. The narrator is unnamed, situating him within a literature of estrangement, and throughout he will deconstruct the facts of the life of one "Hervé Guibert" who we assume is the first-person narrator, but in quotation marks. "I had AIDS for three months. More precisely, for three months I believed I was condemned to die of that mortal illness called AIDS." After these three months, the narrator becomes convinced he could be the first on earth to survive this plague. When it was originally published in France, readers were confused by this demarcation of time—is the author stating that he was actually cured of AIDS, is this a speculative work, a narrative sleight-of-hand? We wonder even now: what does he mean when he dangles this before us this promised salvation? Could we be reading, as Guibert himself suggests, "a genuine science fiction adventure in which [he] shall play the role of a hero"?

DECEMBER 26, 1988

I trace over the years the arrows and asterisks written in the margins on these first pages as I've tried to parse out how time works in this novel. I've written all over this paperback, in pen, pencil, scribbles, and hard-pressed underlining. He begins the book December 26, 1988, in Rome, the day after Christmas. It is now several months, he tells us, after the first three months of his diagnosis where he thought that he was going to die (perhaps there is a die in every diagnosis, as William Gass observed that there is a die in every diary). And now he is writing "several months after those three months when I was truly convinced I was lost, and after the months that followed when I was able to believe myself saved by the luckiest of chances . . ." It takes me years of rereading this opening movement to understand it. Hervé Guibert, why couldn't you have just written one year? It takes 45 pages into the book, to get this confirmation of a precise dating, when he relays the nightmarish scene of getting blood drawn for his pre-AZT check at the Hôpital Claude-Bernard on December 22, less than a week earlier, and the results of which he will be waiting for during the roughly two weeks into 1989 that comprise the majority of the present-tense frame, to see whether his blood count has deteriorated enough to qualify for the current antiviral protocol. The nurse drawing his blood asks him, "How long have you been under observation? I thought for a few moments before replying 'A year.'" I realize upon further rereadings that the book is about the blurriness of a timeline once you become a medical subject. The disorientation, this space of confusion that we are placed in at the opening and throughout, is intentional. AIDS at the time in which Guibert is writing was clouded in rumors and fictions—his survival was speculative fiction.

I AM ALONE

I am alone here and they feel sorry for me, they worry about me, they think I'm not taking good care of myself, so these friends . . . telephone me regularly, compassionately, me—a man who has just discovered that he doesn't like his fellow men, no, I definitely don't like them, I rather hate them instead, and this would explain everything, that stubborn hatred I've always felt, and I'm beginning a new book to have a companion, someone with whom I can talk, eat, sleep, at whose side I can dream and have nightmares, the only friend whose company I can bear at present.

The writer who writes "I am alone" is absurd, Blanchot theorizes in his essay on narrative voice, thinking through Kafka's journals. If you can write "I am alone," you are at least voicing your solitude to an imagined reader. "I'm beginning a new book to have a companion. . . ." Who is keeping the writer company, the book in the process of being written or the future reader? The narrator has isolated himself in Rome, avoiding people "like the plague," including his friends back home in Paris. He has only confessed to a few friends the doom of his diagnosis, just as he only confessed to a few friends that he believes he will be saved. It's like that line opening Georges Bataille's *Guilty*, translated by Bruce Boone: "These notes link me to my fellow humans as a guideline, and everything else seems empty to me, though I wouldn't have wanted friends reading them." The shame of anticipating a friend reading what needs to be—what has to be—an indiscretion, if it's going to reach towards anything like truth. And yet maybe we too, as readers, are the friends who condemn him, or at least are powerless to save his life.

The sporadic texts and emails *just checking in* have mostly stopped—my friends don't want to hear that all day I am consumed with worry, seized by worry, wracked with this, will I miscarry, will the baby be healthy, how can I do this to my body again, when I am too old, how will we afford another baby, we are not making ends meet now, how will I give birth and teach without maternity leave, all day looking up pessimistic statistics online for genetic abnormalities for my *advanced maternal gestational age*, skimming medical studies, all day worrying, weeping all night, they don't want to know about my ambient dread and suspension, I am supposed to be upbeat, excited. That's a good sign! Marie texts me when I reply to her of my volcanic nausea, using the green vomitous emoji. I am afflicted with the absurdity of my life—it was absurdly destructive to have desired a second child, to allow another person to be born in this world, but I did desire this, so intensely, perhaps for my first to have company once I'm dead or during some future apocalypse, now I've gotten what I wanted, what the hell have I done.

I don't tell people about this study, it is private, like this pregnancy.

DECEMBER 26, 2019

The day after Christmas, I go to a new doctor in Midtown, as my ob-gyn has just retired, suddenly closing down her practice. This entire fall I have been disgustingly sick. I worry there's something wrong with me. In October I had something like a parasite, and couldn't keep anything down. Then soon after a persistent respiratory infection that lasted for months, due to an outbreak at my daughter's preschool. The doctor informs me he cannot read the blood work of a pregnant woman. I need an ob-gyn, he says to me, to monitor my hormone levels as sufficiently rising, but it's too early, at six weeks, no one will see me yet. I forgot this ghostly feeling—you don't exist as a pregnant person until you get through the first month or two alone. You could pay out of pocket, people do that, he says to me, but I'm imagining you don't have money if your kid is in the waiting room right now. I don't like him at all, don't like his smug face, don't like when I tell him where I teach, he maintains, correctly, "But you're not full-time, right?" It was that fall that they stopped inviting the part-timers to meetings at the college, unsure if they were going to eliminate them completely, without contracts or a union, they could do that, perhaps why I began getting so sick, somatizing this cruelty. You're overworked, the doctor says to me, in a patronizing, isn't-this-obvious tone, when I tell him about my various commutes teaching, the three classes on three campuses in the fall, my sicknesses of the past years. And he was right, I am overworked, but it was the way he followed it with, "that's all," that disturbed me. Afterwards we stopped inside a salad place nearby which reeked like a cemetery. I had to leave. The last time I had seen a doctor was a month earlier, another pedantic male doctor at the urgent-care clinic the day after Thanksgiving, having woken up with pink eye, still the raging sore throat, the horrible hacking cough over my bed at night that made me wonder if I had broken a rib. Pneumonia, maybe. Could you be pregnant? the X-ray technician asks as a precaution. I mean, I could be. There was that one furtive coupling on the couch a couple days earlier, the only fuck in months of absolute miserabilism. I shuffled to the bathroom in my paper robe, denim overalls at my waist, and peed into a cup. The doctor's gross smirk. Negative. But I wasn't pregnant enough for it to show up on a test. Or the sperm might still have been traveling around inside of me. Growing a life inside of me, apparently, instead of a death.

DEADLINE

The numbered sections read like days. The suspense of a deadline here is linked to the author's mortality. Will the hero die, will the drug of the hour prolong his lifespan for the length of the book, will he instead kill himself? The "plot" of the book, like the sequels that will follow in his illness cycle, traces the shape of a cemetery plot. An actual plot he is certain fans will flock to when he is buried on the island of Elba, he tells us in his follow-up *Compassion Protocol*, written after the previous book has made him famous, a name, synonymous in France with a person with AIDS.

Each drawing of blood heightens the narrative tension. "My blood count continues to deteriorate with each passing day." The opening pages dramatizes the depletion of the narrator's T4 cells, like a game of Pac-Man, "the circulatory system . . . a labyrinth," the virus gobbling up all the "immunological plankton." His last blood work showing his T4 count at 368, when the number drops under 200 it would mean he has developed full-blown AIDS, leaving him vulnerable to fatal secondary infections and qualifying him to take AZT, which was supposed to help slow down the complete assault on his immune system, to give him time. Throughout he is told by Dr. Chandi, his current doctor, that the AZT will extend his life 12–15 months, and if not, he has only months, or weeks, left. "Someone about to start taking AZT is already dead, beyond the hope of salvation."

He must write the book quickly, before he begins taking AZT, to slow down the imminent surrender to death. Throughout the writing of the novel, staged within the novel itself, the narrator holds off taking the antiviral, until after he finishes his book on March 20, when he takes the two blue capsules he has been refusing over these months. Then, he takes it on and off, consulting with others, ultimately deciding not to take it at all, because of severe nausea and headaches. The characteristic digression of the list of side effects of AZT, like a racing pulse.

He gives himself a deadline to tell, as he writes, the story of his illness. Today. Like an On Kawara date painting. "Today, January 4, 1989." Guibert gives himself seven days to write the condensed history of this illness. A week to write a decade. He knows this is impossible. It is a deadline he fails to meet. In seven days he has to call Dr. Chandi to get the results of his blood work over the phone, already in a new stage of his illness where his information has to be given publicly, "propelling me publicly into an openly admitted stage of the disease . . ."

I try to calibrate my own timing for January—scheduling the eight-week scan, the blood work, the *invasive diagnostic tests*, all hopefully before the end of the first trimester. In the opening pages, Guibert writes that he has internalized his work's structure, he has been carrying it along with him, and yet he doesn't know how the book will end—a multiplicity of endings, all porous and premonitory. The narrative will follow "this borderline of uncertainty, so familiar to all sick people everywhere." Although I am not sick. Or I am terribly sick, but it's not seen as a sickness, being temporary, although isn't that the nature of some sickness?

CONTRACTING

It was the fall three years ago, massively pregnant, bouncing on an exercise ball to try to stimulate contractions, trying to not stroke out while watching the presidential debates, the one where he loomed menacingly over her, like a horrible phantom, when I received an email. Would I be interested in writing a short book, a study, about a novel of my choice, for Columbia University Press? I thought I could write it fast in those early months. It took me almost two years before I could even begin thinking through it. Now, I set myself a deadline, amidst the deadline of my body. One month before I find out my news, whether or not I will choose to terminate this pregnancy, whether this pregnancy will decide to end itself, whether it will continue, I will finally write this study of Hervé Guibert.

LIKE A DEAD MAN

It is always in the midst of a medical emergency or crisis of the body when I resume work on it. Perhaps it is when I feel the most isolated that I feel relief returning to the pages of Guibert—the complaint of illness, which is always an experience of isolation. No one can ever really know the experience of your body, an experience worsened by the alienation of medical bureaucracy. The summer before last, I contract shingles, exhausted after having finished a book in a month in order to finally satisfy my contract to my previous publisher and make enough money to pay health insurance and cover rent that summer. Of course, I think immediately to this mirroring with Guibert, like a bodily possession. Guibert, always the unreliable narrator, initially tells us he left his previous doctor, Dr. Nacier, for his gossipy indiscretion as to the celebrities he treated, but really, he tells us, it is because, when diagnosing him with shingles in 1987, he also mentioned that they were seeing a resurgence of this particular variety of chicken pox in seropositive patients, which Dr. Chandi later confirmed, seeing the shingles as diagnostic, even when the narrator was still refusing to be tested, putting in drawers over the years the lab requisitions, either in his name or an assumed one. What is the purpose of knowing, he tells us, the knowledge of which could drive someone like him to suicide? This is repeated, circled around, negated, throughout—Guibert's desire to know or not to know whether or not he was seropositive, and then, once he knew, what that knowledge felt like to experience within the body. Which was, at that time, the knowledge that he was going to die.

I didn't know how to decode the strange symptomry over the past months—headaches, vomiting, diarrhea, the excruciating shoulder blade and rib pain on the left side, along with a painful left breast, scaly, blistered, itchy, a feeling of glass shards within it when Leo sucks. I am up at night weeping, always weeping at night so as not to disturb the child, panicked that I have inflammatory breast cancer, the fastest-growing and most malignant form. I consult with one of those call-a-docs on my shitty marketplace insurance and upload for him a photo of my sad, rashy breast, like the saddest sext ever to have existed. After speaking to me for all of a minute on the phone, the male doctor confidently diagnoses a staph infection and prescribes antibiotics, which do nothing. Finally, I beg my ob-gyn to see me, despite her now not taking my shitty yet still inordinately expensive insurance. Shingles, my doctor says immediately, when I take off my bra. She is arrogant in a way that I always trust from women of authority. She bikes to Manhattan from Brooklyn every day, her sleek bicycle is next to her desk, I imagine her strong thighs wrapped in bike shorts underneath her medical coat. I don't have the correct anatomy for shingles, she says to me, since I'm breastfeeding, ideally the rash would be on the torso, but she is certain she is right. I don't have the peau d'orange—she pronounces it with a French accent, the skin like an orange peel—she's only ever seen one case of it in her twenty-five years of practice.

That summer, it is as if I am afflicted with leprosy and on an island. As I'm trying to write these notes Leo comes in naked, having peed on her practice potty, and climbs into bed, pulls down my white nightgown and nurses. I bicker with John that he should take her, I'm supposed to rest. I mean, I am supposed to rest, but instead I have just begun a secret book. I kick everyone out of bed so that I can heal. Sickness is one of the only times I can attempt to demand my solitude. Perhaps a book is also a solitude, so I can try to be alone. A quote from Kafka in my notes: "I need solitude for my writing, not 'like a hermit'—that wouldn't be enough—but like a dead man."

THE WEEP AND OOZE OF POISON

At my appointment my doctor asks for one week to see if the antiviral works before scheduling a biopsy. By September, I will have better, partially subsidized, though even more outrageously expensive health insurance for at least one year from the college, more if they keep renewing my contract. If I can wait, I could see any doctor within their much wider HMO. How precarious my health has felt, partially because of this instability. I am haunted by the fact that both Susan Sontag and Kathy Acker didn't have health insurance when they were diagnosed with breast cancer. Marie texts to ask how I'm feeling. The check-in feels dutiful, what Guibert in the novel derisively refers to as "friendship's daily bulletins." It's better than late pregnancy, I write to her. It's true, although like then I feel like Job, covered head to toe with boils. It's also better than the postpartum period, the tear ripped through my perineum and anus, a tear between the third and fourth degree, as it's measured, so that I have to sit on a foam donut for weeks, the unbearable hemorrhoids and constipation, like a block of shit trapped inside of me, the crack and burn of sore nipples, the sleeplessness of course but everyone knows that part. I guess I've become accustomed to being rundown. Finally unable to bear the burning pinpricks on my breast, I try the pink calamine lotion John picked up for me. The label on the bottle states that the lotion "dries the oozing and weeping of poison." It strikes me that this is also the potential of writing through the body under capitalism. I take the Guibert into my oatmeal bath, attempt to read a few pages. I feel I understand in a different register Guibert's need to write of doctor's visits and his sick body. A way to not just be a malady to be treated. To be more fully human. Sofia writes me that she longs for "a book that would also be a tonic. Not a course of study but a course of treatment."

In the advanced stage of his illness, his nurses and doctors his only companions, as documented in his sequel *Compassion Protocol*, Guibert writes of finally fulfilling his father's dream of him studying medicine. Already in the first book of his illness, there is a fascination with the virus as a narrative acting upon him. I look up shingles online, caused by the varicella-zoster virus, the same virus that causes childhood chickenpox, living in the body dormant, reactivated in nerves, which feels like a narrative of trauma housed inside of me. There has been no official link made between the postpartum period and shingles, it usually afflicts the elderly, because why would they run studies on the health and mortality of mothers? Yet there are forums online self-diagnosing "postpartum shingles," "shingles and breastfeeding," a pandemic of this, it seems, like so many other postpartum maladies that are ignored, all of these mothers at home, without adequate help, wrung-out, exhausted, unable to get childcare to go to a doctor. I was up at 4:30 a.m. with Leo, as I didn't feed her before she fell asleep last night, we just moved her from car to crib after stealthily putting on her pajamas. Now as I write this she is draining my swollen breast—my armpits still swollen, my ribs tender. With one hand on my phone I look up "swelling" and "shingles." I'm still certain I'm dying, dizzy with this certainty that the shingles are symptomatic of something more severe, will the rash spread, weep, open. The only way I can exist within this borderless state of worry, the velocity of my panic, is by writing in my notebook. Guibert's panicked hypochondria throughout his journals—the almost vertiginous desire towards his death, a "fear and longing." Even at the age of thirty-one, in the translated published diaries, which I read that summer of shingles, smudges all over the massive white paperback, he is obsessed with death, he has various premonitions about contracting what is known then as a gay cancer. "When I am told I am in great shape, and I feel myself dying." I go into the kitchen to take the large stone-blue anti-viral, along with two raw vitamin C tablets and two B-complex capsules recommended to bolster my immune system. I guzzle my horse pills down with yet another cup of coffee, what a paragon of good health I am. Adrenal fatigue, the internet tells me. Wired and tired. Yes, wired and tired wired and tired wired and tired.

CHRONOLOGY OF A BODY

A chronology of a body is not linear. One must piece together dates, doctors, like a detective novel. In October 1983 the narrator's partner Jules is hospitalized at the Cité Universitaire with the fever and swollen lymph nodes beginning to be associated with that "famous plague," whose origins were not narrowed down to being caused by a virus and which was still cloaked in fantastic rumor, for instance that it was a biological weapon launched by Reagan, or that you could get it by sniffing amyl nitrate, although throughout Guibert makes clear that there was at least a strong suspicion it was caused by sharing bodily fluids. At the same time the narrator was returning from Mexico, with a parallel attack of high fever, soon after an abscess appearing at the back of his throat, which made him convinced that they both had AIDS, although they wouldn't get the test for seropositivity until later in the decade. When he becomes certain that he has it, a calm goes over him—the calm of the hypochondriac who has been preparing for a calamity his entire life. "In an instant, this certainty changed everything, turned everything upside down, even the landscape, and this both paralyzed and liberated me, sapped my strength while at the same time increasing it tenfold; I was afraid and light-headed, calm as well as terrified: I had perhaps finally achieved my end."

In the novel Guibert travels in time to the beginning of the decade, a series of portraits, like a rolodex, of incompetent doctors recommended by friends who inflict both absurd examinations as well as ludicrous diagnoses and cures in response to his feeling that something is wrong with him. It is unclear, to both the narrator and the reader, whether these are the confessions of a hypochondriac, as he is often dismissed by these paternalistic doctors, his wandering pain the result of "undoubtedly imaginary ailments that tormented me," including his conviction that he has liver cancer following a case of hepatitis. First he is diagnosed with "benign renal malformation" and told by a urologist to drink large quantities of sparkling water with lemon, then he finally gets an appointment with a homeopath, who his rich and famous friends see several times a week (including Marine, who is based on the actress Isabelle Adjani), and who prescribes a daily intake of dozens of pellets and pills that nearly kill another friend's son, suffering from appendicitis. Guibert's gleeful vivisection of this celebrity quack doctor and his sadistic herbal remedies foisted on mostly female patients:

> [The office] where he conducted his most titillating experiments on his most famous female patients, shutting them up nude inside metal chests after affixing all over their bodies needles filled with concentrates made from herbs, tomatoes, bauxite, pineapples, cinnamon, patchouli, turnips, clay, and carrots, from which lockers they would stagger out as if drunk, and a handsome shade of scarlet.

The doctor prescribes him with spasmophilia, not exactly psychosomatic, as Guibert explains to us, but still involving the unconscious decisions on the part of the patient where to localize his pain. Finally Muzil, the character based on Michel Foucault, recommends another doctor, a "pale, translucent manikin" who diagnoses him with dysmorphophobia, another word for body dysmorphic disorder, an obsessive focus on the flaws of the body that the doctor patronizingly describes as an illness of youth, prescribing him antidepressants. But of course Muzil, who is coughing up a lung that he's medicating with large doses of antibiotics, doesn't take any of his friend's ailments seriously, even though following the dating of the novel the philosopher will only have eight months to live. Eventually, Muzil's cough will become severe enough that he will consult an elderly internist in his neighborhood, who proclaims him in perfect health, just before he collapses unconscious in a pool of blood in his kitchen and must be hospitalized, one month before he dies.

Guibert tries to outline the specific dating of his body's history, a decade of (collective and personal) repression as to how AIDS was transmitted underlined by a constant fear and deferred diagnosis. 1980 was the year of hepatitis. 1987 was his shingles. By the next year the "revelation" of his illness, which he tells us in a later hallucinatory Genet-like passage he suspects he contracted on a dancefloor in Mexico after being kissed by an "old whore," the raw white wound later appearing in his throat (some less-than-latent misogyny there, to assume that he contracted the virus from the kiss of a woman portrayed as a Felliniesque succubus, despite chronicling his unprotected sex throughout the decade). "That's the chronology that becomes my outline, except whenever I discover that progression springs from disorder."

TO THE FRIEND

The title of Guibert's novel provides some of the suspense. Who is his addressee? Is it the friends who are either dead or dead to him because of past treacheries? He connects the constellation of his famous circle all somehow linked to the early onset of what in France was called *le sida*, which was mired in paranoia and conspiracies. He is telling the narrative of a body and a disease, through gossip and the experience of himself and his intimates, an act of revenge, to all who didn't save him.

Last night, dinner with my former editor and his wife. Maybe don't tell him you have shingles, John suggests beforehand, which irritates me. Yes, best not to talk about something so unsightly as the goings-on of my leaky body over a professional dinner between old friends. But by the way my editor jokes nervously when his wife brings up the practice of at-home postpartum pelvic floor therapy in France, the government pays for it there, how humane!—"Well, I wouldn't know about that"—that makes me realize John was probably right. My editor wanted me to bring the whole family, wanted to meet the baby, who they both smiled at expectantly. I've known them now for years, but it's difficult, near impossible, to truly feel like friends when there's such a power imbalance. I need to sell the novel, which I have pulled from my previous publisher, to this editor, now at a more prestigious publishing house, in order to pay for preschool for the year, pay rent for yet another summer when we're not teaching, to pay off the taxes I still owe from the last advance, and it's only going to pay for part of all of that. I'm putting on quite the performance, and he knows it. How has your identity changed since having a child? he asks me, as I burn all over, squirm in my seat, pretend I'm not uncomfortable. It's gotten so much easier in these past years to pretend my body is not uncomfortable. It also feels impossible to have conversations about children when one side doesn't have any, nor inclination or experience. For it's boring and constant, a different way of life, taking care of others—but also so bodily, even often joyful. The self changes, it's an uncomfortable stretch, especially for a writer, to never be alone again, and yet also so full of abundance. But also my life feels more private now—I don't wish to broadcast the mess of my domesticity, at least to him, right now. It's my mess. Still I answer to appease him. I make my pitch. I tell him I'm writing a lot now because of alienation, alienation stimulates me, as an adjunct, a mother, a writer, perhaps a need to have a voice in opposition to overdetermined narratives . . . I go home and feel wrenched, wretched, at how I'm always needing to pitch my self. Later that day I hear back from Sofia: You are far too miserable, she writes sweetly, to be considered a sellout. Anyway, writers whoring for cash is a venerable tradition!

ROOM

There are 100 sections in *To the Friend Who Did Not Save My Life*. Guibert referred to them as rooms. Entering them, we can access the solitude and intimacy of this work, witness the performance and endurance of the body while writing the novel within the work. Are these days? Writing sessions?

The next day, hot and fuzzy, a metallic taste in my mouth from the antivirals. I am not resting as I should be. I am working on revisions of the manuscript—always another revision, just as Guibert writes of revising a manuscript in *To the Friend*. I want to be rid of it, like being cured of it. Leo runs around naked, climbing on me, nursing. Twice today she squatted and laid a turd, once on the rug, luckily solid, then a softer one on the wooden floor. And now, later in the afternoon, I only have fifteen minutes to think before the babysitter leaves. I beg for fifteen clear minutes to read a couple pages of the Guibert, to write these lines in my notebook. The door open so she doesn't cry for mommy. During the hour the babysitter has been here I have corralled Leo to pee on her practice potty, then cleaned it up. The babysitter leaves her food everywhere—her half-eaten apple, her half-finished ravioli she brought with. I walk around like a mom or maid cleaning after both of them. Finally I entice them to go on the porch to blow bubbles.

BHANU

On her blog Bhanu posts about a line from César Aira in *The Paris Review*: "The novel requires an accumulation of time, a succession of different days: without that, it isn't a novel." What does this say, Bhanu asks, about the labor of caretaking? If a writer takes care of others, or must take care of themselves, time is of course disrupted. She writes: "Without these days, in succession, can a person be a novelist?" I read the original essay. "You cannot write a novel the night before dying," writes Aira. But isn't that what Guibert was doing? Writing novels the night before dying? Early on in his diaries, years before his diagnosis: "It's death that drives me (that would be the end of the book)." In many ways Guibert is more of a diarist than a novelist. The diary feeling is a shape of fragmented consciousness. Then what does he mean when he writes in *Compassion Protocol*, a classic aphoristic flourish closing a section, "It is when what I am writing takes the form of a journal that I most strongly feel that I am writing fiction"?

ROME

Earlier this December, when I am still thinking about thinking about my Guibert study, I meet up with a celebrated novelist who blurbed my forthcoming novel. We speak about our love for Guibert, the only writer I talk to any writer about lately, probably because I haven't been reading much of anyone else. The boring-ness of someone else's obsession, like tunnel vision. She has writ-ten a novella set in Elba, thinking about Napoleon's exile there, and spends a good portion of each year in Italy. She didn't know that Elba was where Guibert made his vacation home, that he's buried there, that Elba is where he filmed his final diary film, *La Pudeur ou l'Impudeur (Modesty, or Immodesty)*. Oh you must go to Elba, she says to me. It's so kid-friendly. This writer I am having coffee with is younger than me. She doesn't have children. She has a tenured position in a prestigious writing program. She says something about how important it is to have a pilgrimage when writing a book, to have that object of obsession to gestate on in the landscape. I mean, I agree with her. And I know she is try-ing to be encouraging. We are both lovers of Sebald, so it makes sense. But I am reminded of Anamarie's joke about Sebald's *Rings of Saturn*, I don't trust anyone who has time for a walking tour of Suffolk!

Everyone tells me to go to Italy to write this book. That fall I even applied for another part-time ("guest") faculty grant to get $1,000 approved towards the trip, not that that was enough. That's what I fantasized about when I agreed to do this book—the December after Leo turned two, after the semester was out, I'd go to Rome by myself, and this is how I'd wean her. I'd meditate on the hardness of my breasts, the time-bomb of my breasts, while thinking through Guibert's slippery memoir of the body. The first time I planned for this trip, I told myself I'd write the study in a month. Then the plan was I'd go this December, by myself, when Leo turned three, maybe I could even write it in a week, high off of my own aching and delirious solitude, that's all the time I'd really have. It's now nearing the end of December and I am still trying to wean her—she still nurses quickly when she wakes up and goes to bed, occasionally at naptime, there's almost no milk, she just takes a quick sip, which calms her. I still have never traveled without her. It seems like Marie constantly travels to Europe or Los Angeles alone. I can't or won't or haven't figured out how to. Why is everyone telling a mother of a toddler to go to Rome? I haven't gone to a movie by myself in years. And what would I do in Rome? I'd go to Rome with a partner and toddler, just like the brief weekend in Paris now more than a year ago—I wouldn't be able to read or write in Rome. We'd wait in exhausting lines at museums. I can go to Rome but I cannot go to Rome alone, I cannot go to Rome for this book. There would be nothing romantic or at least solitary about going to Rome. We'd eat pasta and take photos of Leo. I cannot go to Rome and I cannot really be alone. Except when I am sick. Except here. In this book.

COHERENCE

That summer, Bhanu writes me she has been reading through contemporary autofiction in translation, Knausgaard, Édouard Louis, Annie Ernaux. I'm making a study of coherence, she writes me. The extreme confidence of these writers, in the status of their art form, she writes, I'm obsessed with cracking the code of this security. Is it cultural? Is it simply this, that their work as writers is valued? She read Guibert's journal some years ago, which is distinct from what she is studying now, she writes, "the surface, the commerce, the fold." I live for Bhanu's emails, which are as alive with her genius as all of her other writing. She's right about everything, of course, except I'm not sure that Guibert is distinct from the rest, except that he's seen as more sacred because he's dead. Guibert hoped for *To the Friend* to be a commercial bestseller, as Mathieu Lindon writes in his memoir. In the novel, his acidic tribute to his former editor, Lindon's father, Jérôme Lindon of Les Editions de Minuit, describing the meeting where Guibert tries to negotiate an advance for the diary manuscript, as well as payment for outstanding royalties. The editor, "that wonderful man" (this is extreme Guibert bile), tells him to write a big novel instead with characters, at least then reviewers could summarize the plot in their reviews and anyhow his books don't sell well . . . "Get it in your head once and for all that I am not your father!" Partially as a result of this falling out, Guibert leaves Les Editions de Minuit and sells *To the Friend* to the larger Gallimard. Guibert's novel becomes a bestseller in France, mostly because of the controversy of outing Michel Foucault as dying from AIDS, as well as its distinction as the first memoir by a person living with AIDS. It sells 350,000 copies by 1994. He becomes a media celebrity, appears on the talk show *Apostrophes*. This is the type of attention a writer is supposed to achieve, talk show attention.

SURVIVAL ENERGY

In my notes this quote, I realize later it is Blanchot—"At some point the writer—perhaps because of financial constraints or other pressures—pronounces the end and then the artist pursues the unfinished matter elsewhere." One publishes, perhaps, because one must. How much were the illness books a form of financial anxiety? Is that partially why they were written, and with such speed? Later in the novel, the narrator has another publishing meeting to get an advance on the contract for his next book, possibly this book we are reading, which he will need to travel "around the world in an iron lung or blow my brains out with a golden bullet."

It was Bhanu who first used the phrase "survival energy" with me. This was the end of September after I had shingles, I was in despair because my former editor had initially rejected the novel after I was given the strong impression that he was going to buy it. *Brilliant but don't have larger vision to publish it, etc. Need to make certain numbers.* I heard these pat phrases through my now-former agent the morning of Christine Blasey Ford's testimony, and then the blustery wounded yelling of Brett Kavanaugh's on the radio, his pointing to the objectivity of his dumb fucking calendar, versus the ephemerality of her memories. *Sorry to give you terrible news when the country . . .* I had just taken Leo to get her passport, buying a pair of bulb-like Yohji trousers I now couldn't afford, and couldn't afford anyway, for the panel on "Writing the Body" in London, as I thought I was selling a book. I use my two hours of babysitting time that only occurs once or twice a week to sit in my office, which isn't even my office anymore, and put my head down on the desk. A photograph of the author at work (weeping). The next day I take the train to the city and get my hair all cut off while having to bounce Leo on my lap. It doesn't look pretty. I don't care, particularly. I wanted some way to grieve. My hairstylist is reading *King Kong Theory*, she tells me. I can't read male voices right now, she then says. I agreed. I'm so sick of male voices. Certain types of male voices anyway—their arrogance and smugness. Then why write a study now of Hervé Guibert? Although I can't group in my Hervé with that classification, perhaps his queerness and positive status separates him from that category of male voices, although it is undeniable that he moved in a rarefied and exclusionary social circle.

I read somewhere on the internet yesterday, that the vote for Kavanaugh's nomination was on a woman's right to exist. Perhaps this was my vote, on my right to exist as a writer. At least here, in this city. I thought that publishing, that these institutions, would support me somehow, love me, as opposed to what they always do, which was fatigue and sicken me. Did I allow myself to be pushed into this, since I have had a child? For if I refuse (to apply for fellowships, and teaching jobs I know I won't get, to pitch books to larger publishers), I am stating I have, or at least my work has, little value. All that week in full crisis mode with John over our future. His desire to go back to a full-time library job in order for us to have regular benefits, which for me would mean mommy jail again, when I was so miserable that first year. It's not like I wouldn't have to teach then, I just wouldn't be able to do the deep thinking required to do my work, even once Leo went to preschool. Making lunch in the morning, the drop offs, the pick-ups.

"Kate, it's possible to write without resources," Bhanu writes me. "But after a while, survival energy takes up the day and the night and the life." Does this mean she's not a writer as well?

Bhanu then asks me, because she's never been awarded a grant, a residency, a fellowship, a prize, a lucrative publishing deal? All of these gatekeepers who rejected my novel, all white, almost entirely cisgendered, male, straight. The institutions of capitalism and white supremacy, which I too have profited from, although never enough to have any stability, to be able to have time, to stop working constantly and for not enough pay.

THE WOUNDED MAN

That fall while reading Guibert on the train, when we were still taking trains, I also look at myself through my phone's camera, mesmerized by the new severity of my face, the flat line my mouth makes now. I research skincare on my phone—for pleasure, for it is a form of pleasure—the desired layers of serums, creams, all pushed into the skin with massage tools, fingers, make plans for how I will afford a microcurrent tool, once I sell the book, that will send jolts of electricity through my facial muscles. The cruelty of Guibert's portrait of Marine, inspired by the famous actress Isabelle Adjani, whose youthful beauty he previously photographed, her ponytailed profile while watching a tiger through the bars at a zoo, leaning against bars, laying down, always posed, pouting, part of Marine's obsession with, Guibert writes, "endlessly multiplying her face." All the rumors later of Adjani's Botox addiction, that she ruined her perfect face. The other whisper campaign, once she moved to the States, which coincided with the height of AIDS hysteria, that she was dying of the virus or had cancer, or was already dead. In the novel Guibert memorializes his former friend ambivalently, like a spurned lover, and repeats many of the same rumors, making the novel something like a tabloid work, reflective of the gossip of the time. It is money, too, that separates the narrator from Marine. He counted on Marine to act in his film scenario based on her, she agreed to take the role, but then wouldn't let him sell the screenplay, based on her life. "I'd modeled my main character on her, filching certain aspects of her life, such as her neurotic attitude towards her own image." He needed the money to quit journalism. Marine could have made him rich and famous—protected somehow—and she failed him. Because of this treachery, like the treachery of his editor, he wishes that she had the disease, but also so they could share, he writes, a blood bond forever. He wishes she'd die of it! I watch on YouTube the 1984 César awards that he fictionalizes in these passages (the translation calls it the Academy Awards, annoying me, why should translations act like all novels take place in the States?). Jack Nicholson reads her name from an envelope. Adjani all in white feathers. The magnificence of her heavily made-up face. *Merci, merci beaucoup*, she says prettily, breathlessly. In Guibert's revenge-play, "She appeared in a god-awful white dress looped with pearls, wearing her hair in a frumpy bun, and tottering on too-high heels with her fur piece awry like a drunken Mae West, when she wasn't even thirty years old yet, a dress that screamed bad luck, in my opinion . . ." And yet in real life there were rhinestones, not pearls, on her dress. Pan to the crowd, I try to squint—is Hervé there? Ah, there he is later, in another clip, on stage in a tuxedo, accepting for best original screenplay, for *L'homme blessé*, which he wrote with Patrice Chéreau. *The Wounded Man*.

That fall of October 1983, Marine's new play has opened, which Guibert depicts as a catastrophe that further isolates her, on the verge of a nervous breakdown possibly spurred on by those around her for publicity, already rumors of her deteriorating health. His cruel portrait recalls a Francis Bacon painting. "Marine looked like a frantic monkey screeching and battering herself against the bars of her cage." The cruelty is always undercut with the tenderness of love, however ambivalent. After her breakdown, the narrator visits her in the hospital, they laugh together, old friends. He is consumed by a passion seeing her there with her wrists bandaged to paint her in a copy of Gabriel von Max's portrait of the ecstatic virgin Anna Katharina Emmerich, as always obsessed with nineteenth-century realism. I look up the painting online, marks of stigmata reported on her body in early 1813, the periodic bleeding of her hands and feet. The blue pallor of the gauze wrapped around her head, of her skin. As I write this, I have just gotten a text from Marie, who finally has read my novel that's now coming out, having been revised to the hilt and finally accepted by the editor. Marie, an Isabelle Adjani obsessive, continually posts her images on her Instagram, especially stills from *Queen Margot*, when the nearly forty-year-old actress's face is slightly frozen and yet still lovely. I was surprised to find things about me in your novel that were unkind, Marie wrote (but of course her name is not Marie, don't ask!). I didn't know what to say. I wanted to write, "of course, she's a character, she's not you," but knew that would not satisfy her, don't even know if that was the truth. In the novel I wrote of her wealth, how she had a night nanny, her immaculate slenderness, even when pregnant, how she was always flying to Paris or Los Angeles despite having two small children. Maybe I was bitchy—if an acknowledgment of class angst is bitchy—but I don't think I was unkind. Nothing like Guibert's mean portrait of Adjani. And yet in *Compassion Protocol*, which I began reading that fall, he responds to a friend calling him unkind, "But I myself do not think my books are unkind. I certainly feel that they are shot through by—among other things—truth and falsehood, treachery, by this theme of unkindness, but I would not say they are fundamentally unkind."

BITCHY PROSE

When I was in conversation with Clutch at the New York Public Library, now nearly a year ago, when the library was still open, we chatted about our love for *slutty* (their term) prose around a community, like Bruce Boone's *Century of Clouds* or Audre Lorde's *Zami*, formative works for both of us. A question from the audience—how do we wrangle with the ethics of writing friendships? I bring up Guibert, who Clutch and I always refer to, in our conversations, which used to be regular, and now it's been too long, I wonder how they are. My desire to be bitchier than I let myself be, to be closer to truth, not to be cruel, but to write the truth of schisms within community, in fact this is how literary communities function, the exquisite difficulty and fragility of friendships with others. I wonder now, is it his candor that drives me to Hervé Guibert? That he says what he's not supposed to, in the quest for truth, as opposed to so much of the first-person now, that's supposed to be incredibly earnest and moral (more so in nonfiction, fiction still allows, perhaps, ambivalent or amoral narrators). What attracts me to Guibert is his Nietzschean spirit of *ressentiment*, of trying to seek not only truth, but also to expose treachery, to get his revenge. It is the pettiness of Guibert that thrills me, the intimacy of the malice in the voice, which intersects with how much of the work could be read as gossip or rant. When he learns that he is dying, or at least that the clock has started, or is ticking louder than before, he does not become more gracious and centered, he does not listen to meditation tapes nor make amends—his fangs come out. What an asshole, Anamarie texts me, jokingly, when I tell her I can't schedule a playdate with our daughters, I'm still working on the Guibert. She still hasn't, she said, forgiven him for what he writes about his mother in *Ghost Image*, about how the beauty of women fades past the age of forty. Yes, I want to say. He's such an asshole! What an asshole! There's something thrilling about this, about his sheer vindictiveness, about eschewing politeness, it's so foreign to how women are supposed to be in public. Another friend writes me, one who asked me not to name her, well the only reason Guibert wrote what he did is because Foucault was dead, and Guibert knew he'd soon be dying, otherwise he would have refrained. You don't know Guibert at all! I want to say. But I don't. I only say it here. See, I'm too nice in real life!

What is the space of literature for, if not as a scratching pad for our irritants? I keep going back to the one English editor who, when rejecting my book over email, said that my novel was irritating for him, especially the complaints of the pregnant narrator, although perhaps he was just revealing his prejudices, he said, his horror of children. I'm tired, anyway, he wrote me, of the conventions of autofiction. This is how he rejected me. "I'm tired of the conventions of autofiction." I too find at least the term *autofiction* annoying, just as Guibert and Duras were annoyed by how the term was projected upon their work, where in France at the time, it was used by critics to make sense of how a work could be at once fiction and autobiographically derived, first coined by Serge Doubrovsky in relation to his 1977 novel *Fils*, and now it was dubiously back in fashion, I think, to signal a discomfort with first-person narratives passing themselves off as fiction. Many contemporary critics fail to understand that the term *autofiction* suggests slipperiness, an estrangement of the I-narrator, who may or may not have the same name as the author, so that the space of the work can become a space of freedom. For what if, what if, I was trying to be an irritant? Where is the role in contemporary literature for the irritants, the petty, the gossips, the haters? Because in real life I thanked the editor for his thoughts, knowing the power that he still held over me, or the power at least that I felt that he held over me, the prestige attached to his name versus mine, the possibility that he could change his mind, or publish me someday, or that if I acted unprofessional by being leaky in any way, that would somehow brand me as difficult in the publishing world, which would then take away my ability to attempt to make a living by piecing together adjunct work and contracts, always renewed every year after I complete my supplications, but here, in the space of a work I only know one will read, for it's only one reader reading at a time, or perhaps no one will read, what does it matter, I am already dead, I can say what I'm thinking, and feeling, that I wept in the adjunct office when I got his email, and then had to put on a face for my straight male student who was enthralled by the work of a particular male writer of autofiction published by this same press, I wanted to say, is he so tired when his friend does it so prestigiously, and that I felt this rejection deeply for some time.

SUCCESS AND FAILURE

When my book is rejected everywhere, I jot down a quote from the diaries: "it is perhaps preferable to circle around the idea of the novel, to dream it . . . and to botch it, rather than succeed, since the successful novel is perhaps a very banal form of writing." I wonder when I submit to full-scale revisions of the novel, the months and months of trying to make everything perfect, nothing too difficult, whether I'm getting further and further away from the moment of process, the private impulses, that I was hoping to document. It is the failure of Guibert's novel that interests me—the rushed, passionate, desperate, furious character of it. As opposed to all of the polished turds being published now.

BIRTHDAY

Yesterday was my birthday, December 30, which I could not bring myself to record, even though I worked on the shingles section for an hour or so, rereading my diaries from that time. Pregnant at forty-two. Like those Kerch terracotta figurines of the pregnant crone Bakhtin uses for his concept of the grotesque body in his study on Rabelais. Hervé Guibert attempted suicide the day before his thirty-sixth birthday—he survived, yet died two weeks later, his damaged heart giving out. We say AIDS or AIDS-related illness and it's become almost a shorthand to not access what that means, the true horror of that, the consequences of that, in history, in literature, in life. He should have been alive now. He should have lived longer. He should have written more. He was thirty-six when he died. Only thirty-six. Not even middle-aged. The morbid calculations I make now. He would have been sixty-four now. His friend Sophie Calle who was born in 1953 is now sixty-five. Chris Kraus is sixty-four, born in 1955. Dennis Cooper is sixty-six. Kevin Killian, who just died, was sixty-six. David Wojnarowicz would have been sixty-five— he died at thirty-eight.

For a while I labored under the misapprehension that Guibert was like me a Capricorn. Although December 14 meant he was actually a Sagittarius. I only realized this once I had begun this project, formally, on the anniversary of his death. For a while I thought I would begin the project by getting Guibert's birth charts read, even though, being from the Midwest, I don't know anything about astrology. But then I think I forgot, or gave up the idea, as I didn't know how to go about doing such a thing. But I wonder now, can you make a chart for a death day?

SLEEPLESS NIGHTS

It is now New Year's Day. I am sitting upright, forcing myself to write this scrap, after a sleepless night. Leo stayed in bed with us because of the incessant fireworks, I slept on a sliver of the bed, or I hardly slept at all, woke up with a headache, a sore throat so that I don't want to drink water let alone coffee. I have to shower, I haven't left the house for two days, we have agreed to go over to a friend's apartment so our children can play together, a new ritual for us, the social playdate. We are picking up Italian pastries first. I will probably eat all of them. Everyone else will demur, because it's New York. That is my new diet—pastries, pancakes, toast. I have at most fifteen minutes to write this passage. This passage will not be great literature. It will announce, perhaps—I existed today. I survived. An hour a day, if I am lucky. A clear hour if I am very lucky. Leo is coughing in her sleep as my staccato accompaniment.

The will it takes Guibert to write a page when sick and exhausted. The numbering of passages makes this more immediate. "My book is battling the fatigue created by the body's struggles against the attacking virus." A book that reads as an exhausted body. He can only have four good hours of work a day, he writes in the novel. By the next book he will have even less time. A work that accumulates out of an exhausted life, out of the narrative momentum of survival energy, is by its nature fragmented, coming in starts and stops, manifested out of any available time.

SPEED OF LIGHT

The dying narrator experiences a form of time travel—he finds himself in a quickly aging body in his thirties. That line from Chris Marker's *La Jetée*— "He understood" there was no way to escape Time, and that this moment he had been granted to watch as a child, which had never ceased to obsess him, was the moment of his own death. All Muzil wants to know when he learns he is dying, without most likely being told the specifics—"How long?" Is this why I'm writing so much? This drive? Is it fear? Hypochondriac energy? The desire to write all the books I have planned, as quickly as possible. People are suspicious, I should slow down. What is this itch? Some reaction to the ghostliness of family and work? As a way to exist? I measure this recent, almost compulsive, work ethic against the proliferation of literary productivity in Guibert's final years. All the books since his diagnosis, each narrative with the suspense of a new drug that would keep him alive for long enough to finish the book or the alternative—death, fantasized as self-inflicted, a fate he would fulfill halfway. From his diagnosis at the end of 1988 until his death in 1991, he wrote *To the Friend Who Did Not Save My Life*, and then the follow-ups, *Compassion Protocol, The Man in the Red Hat*, and a hospital diary, *Cytomegalovirus*. Between 1977 and 1990 he published seventeen books, and then five other books were published posthumously, more if you include the diaries. The narrator writes of Muzil's endless book, but he could also be referring to his own work, the novels, the diaries, writings that document an abbreviated life. A friend is editing another of his manuscripts throughout the book, and is annoyed with the narrator how rushed the book feels, like a rough draft. And the book we are reading too, that he dramatizes writing in front of us, has a quality of speed. There is something almost underwritten about it, as if from the momentum to shake oneself out of severe fatigue. I wonder how this relates to Italo Calvino's aesthetic of "quickness," in his *Six Memos for the Next Millenium*, an inner propulsion furthered by digressions and repetitions, circling around an object in the narrative, a mode of contracting time that attempts to represent the agility of a thinking mind. Even this work I am writing now, thinking through Guibert, I know it isn't perfect, but I have to write it now, or it's not going to happen, I need to push it out as if through my body, I need to just put down my thinking on the matter, even if the thinking is fickle, even if it changes over time, even if I repeat myself. His friend doesn't understand, Guibert writes, that the work for him has become one of condensed time, the desire to write an entire life that will now be cruelly reduced, to write with "the speed of light," there is no time now for the slow and retrospective:

> . . . when I learned I was going to die, I'd suddenly been seized with the desire to write every possible book—all the ones I hadn't written yet, at the risk of writing them badly: a funny, nasty book, then a philosophical one—and to devour these books almost simultaneously in the reduced amount of time available, and to devour time along with them, voraciously, and to write not only the books of my anticipated maturity but also, with the speed of light, the slowly ripened books of my old age.

NIGHT AND FOG

The past two days I've been too sick and exhausted to work on this study, except for rearranging my notes from previous years. I have had no appetite but I need to eat something constantly, to get rid of the foul taste in my mouth, so I subsist entirely on ginger candy, popsicles, bagels, hard-boiled eggs. My fatigue and nausea have absented me of all personality. And yet it's supposed to be a sign, perversely, that things are proceeding well. I take hard naps on the couch all day, getting up only to read a book to Leo, to build blocks with her, sitting on the floor at her insistence when all I want to be doing is lying down. I have had to wean Leo quickly, in the past week, we've plied her with sweets and hot chocolate in order to cope. I began to experience what I read online is called an *extreme nursing aversion* that can happen especially when pregnant—the thought of having anything else drained from me feels impossibly hideous. At least I will now get my body back, I joke to John. My breasts are already full, preparing for another years-long residence.

At night I cannot sleep. Last night I laid there and listened to the mice in the walls. The sonic devices I purchased online are supposed to drive them away—yet at first they drive them crazy. It's supposed to be more humane than traps or poison. The one solo scratch from the nights before has become something like a torturous symphony. Mice in the walls behind my head; mice in the ceiling. At 4 a.m. on the couch to which I had retreated, unable to stand the noise in the bedroom, I heard something like shrieking or scrambling.

I wake up with my face puffy and swollen, attempting the ice roller to try to outline a face again. All the weeping bouts, due to the sudden weaning, like the bottom has dropped out—the sudden absence of prolactin and oxytocin (the love hormone), mixed with my skyrocketing pregnancy hormones. This morning Leo brought out her plastic medical kit and gave me a check-up—using a plastic tube to fill my body with imaginary saline, using a cotton pad to wipe down a vein before giving me a shot, pressing hard into my flesh with her needleless syringe. All good, Kate, she says to me.

Perhaps the strangeness and impossibility of being a pregnant body while weaning is the ideal state to write a study about Guibert, Sofia writes in response to my wretched report. And it's true, this study will have to proceed swiftly, like a performance at the body's limits. I will have to proceed at the risk of these parallels, the different stakes of these exhaustions—life and death. The risky parallels Guibert makes as well—his *Night and Fog* comparison, worrying his gaze is like a doomed camp inmate, his own body "an Auschwitzian exhibit" in the sequel. I don't want to state that my exhaustion approximates or even comes close to mirroring that of an AIDS patient. I want only to describe my exhausted body at work, writing in a room, while contemplating the exhaustion and illness of another body, writing in a room. But these two differing states do change things, Sofia writes me. The battle against death justifies and demands writing, devoting oneself to one's art. But art is seen as taking the mother away from her child— she is not supposed to write through her exhaustion—art is the great time-stealer, the life-sucker. Art, writes Sofia, then becomes something indecent—like a crime.

PROTECT PROTECT

In early January, I am shocked by the news that Elizabeth Wurtzel, famous for her defiantly unfiltered first person, died of breast cancer, *after a long battle* (always, says Sontag, the military metaphor). I text Suzanne, panicked. Wurtzel was only fifty-two. Suzanne's mother died from breast cancer at forty-seven. My mother died from cancer at fifty-five. We commiserate over our history of shitty insurance plans, of rarely seeing doctors. I am always at risk of losing my health insurance every year if I do not get asked back at the college, where I still have to pay into it thousands a month for a family HMO plan that consumes nearly two-thirds of my wages. If I had a miscarriage today I would have to go to the ER, I wrote Suzanne. She just got a mammogram in a public clinic. I haven't been able to get a mammogram since turning forty, as they don't want to give mammograms to breast-feeding people, and now I'm pregnant again. Will we survive this scary decade? The cancer phobia really began when my daughter was born, when I considered the horror of disappearing from her life, I wouldn't even be a memory, only photographs, a ghost. I read Wurtzel's op-ed from years back in the *New York Times* about testing positive for the BRCA mutation, one that women of Ashkenazi descent are 10 times more likely to have, but insurance won't cover the test, unless breast cancer has already been diagnosed in you or a primary family member. I spend time on the phone with a cancer genetics counselor—we can't give you the test when you're pregnant she says. Why? I've been here five years and we've never done it, she says. I am forty-two, I try to explain to her, I am probably perimenopausal, the exact risk group for these cancers, my mother died of small-cell lung cancer, which is BRCA-related. I don't know any women in my extended family on my mother's side, save for the estranged half-sister I haven't seen since the funeral more than fifteen years ago. My mother's family is all Jews from the Bronx who then moved to Florida. But since she was estranged from her family by the time I was born, I have no idea how any of them died. An ovarian cyst was spotted on my ultrasound days earlier. I am told I have to wait until after the pregnancy to get it checked out. And then what? I will be too exhausted to seek care. How will I have time, with a baby and a toddler, to get preventative checkups? I will be taking care of my body, which has just been brutalized, while trying to keep a very small being who's also been through trauma alive and fed through my mangled body, while comforting yet another small being. Insurance doesn't pay for a follow-up after birth until six weeks. That's what the tech said to me as well, gliding the gel over my belly—as I watched her draw a shape over the cyst on my ovary, the small little globule inside the other sac of my uterus, these abstract shapes within shapes—as we waited for the heartbeat. Is it dead, I kept on saying to the tech, anxiously, looking at the little globule. How morbid I have been lately. The punctuation of the tiny heartbeat through the small soft sac-shape. Strong and fast, this heartbeat doubled inside me. You should wait until after the baby comes to get it checked out. But really it's not that I should wait, it's that I will need to wait, no one will see me for anything other than this pregnancy. I go home and worry like a ribbon slowly unspooling from me. Is this the same ovarian cyst that the ultrasound found at the dating scan almost four years ago, or a new one? I can't figure out how to get the records from my retired ob-gyn. I can't get a mammogram now that I'm pregnant, and I couldn't get one before because I was breastfeeding. I can't do anything about this cyst. I can't even get a genetics test because I'm pregnant. Is it because the fetal DNA is swimming with my own? I can't understand the science of it, or rather I can't get answers to what seem like basic questions. Is it that they don't know what good having this information might be, while pregnant, as they wouldn't treat me anyway and it would be too late for termination, since the test takes possibly months to return? Because why hold this information in the body? I'm either dismissed or treated as if I am acting difficult whenever I assert any bodily agency or advocate for my own health, and this is always magnified when I'm pregnant, when I'm only supposed to be worried about the fetus. Pregnancy is protective, Suzanne writes, trying to calm me. That's what everyone says. I've been venting to her all morning. What a nightmare, she sympathizes. I have resources—I have some resources!—and it's like they just don't care if I die. I am supposed to protect this fetus, but who protects me? I'm just a vessel. A shell. I'm just supposed to keep alive.

BODY DREAD

One day in the near future when I have an hour, I attempt to return from submergence into my own body dread back to the body of Guibert, the body of his book. I attempt once again to slowly read such a fast book. It reads like the panic of a diagnosis. The body as a site of mystery and horror. What is the suspense? Will he survive? Will he commit suicide? Consulting his appointment book from 1987, the narrator remembers that it was when he found the white papillomas on his tongue that he realized the truth, or, as he phrases it throughout, he goes to a further stage of awareness of his illness, a symptom treated by Dr. Chandi with a sickly yellow coating of anti-fungal medication, following the pattern of treating each symptom without the certainty of the diagnosis, although they both knew that the time had come to be tested, and he began to limit his physical contact, he writes, with only two, one who was aware of his illness (assumedly Jules), and the other who was not (I'm assuming the character he later calls The Poet). In January of 1988 the narrator and Jules finally take the test, partially to convince themselves they were being paranoid. They decided to have the test done anonymously, as was the convention of the time, for, Guibert writes, both personal and professional reasons, namely, he writes, to be able to still cross the border into Italy. This entire pages-long passage is spiked with dread, a narrative spiraling around also going to the Institut Alfred-Fournier for blood analysis to ascertain the progress of the virus, a hospital previously used for treating syphilis patients, as it was already a foregone conclusion they were positive, the description of the nurses snapping on latex gloves there, making sure to throw away the blood-stained cotton. The awful scene of the narrator realizing Jules had fainted, once being dealt this fate, a realization "that when this certainty became official, even though it remained anonymous, it became intolerable." Afterwards they go together to get fireworks for Jules' children, such an awful, tender way to end the section of their devastation. What follows is mired in the collective suffering between the narrator and Jules, as they fall into a giant existential abyss. They don't tell Jules's wife Berthe at first that they are doomed, they keep this secret from her, they all share kisses the New Year's Eve before, showing the deep affection and solidarity between their family unit, although even that scene is shot through with dread, as Guibert, writing with the public knowledge and fears of his time, thinks that the virus is communicated through saliva. Something of these passages of Guibert expressing his love and devotion to his family, sealed by this common fate of blood with them, or so they assumed, is reminiscent of Muzil speaking of the "new complicities, new tenderness, new solidarities" in the San Francisco bathhouses, although fraught more with ambivalence and shame: "still my love for them was a potential bloodbath, into which I plunged them with terror." He prays for the children despite not believing in God, he tells us, all he wants to do is shower them with gifts, silk dresses and toy cars. Their fate hangs over the rest of these passages, like premonitory dread, as Berthe and the children, who Guibert frames as the innocents, suffer unknowingly from a bout of fever and illness, although it turns out only to be the flu that's been going around.

DEATH SENTENCES

The infectiously long sentences in Guibert may be most pronounced in the scenes of medical panic. He tells an interviewer, of these sentences, "They are like escalating fevers, outbursts." He is writing, he tells us in the novel, "a work of imitative fiction that is actually a kind of essay on Thomas Bernhard." A desire to write a Bernhardian book that is in its way a virus—a copy that hijacks cells. The repetition of certain phrases and lines. Repetition as a battering or wearying force. A desire to outdo the rapturous misanthropy of a Bernhard narrator, to be not humane but a Great Hater. His Rome is the Rome of *Extinction*, the last of Thomas Bernhard's novels, where the narrator Murau is in self-exile. Bernhard himself who wrote "fake, disguised essays" on everyone from Glenn Gould to Tintoretto. While writing this book he is possessed by the hypnotic cadence of his (their) sentences, his (their) digressive speed, how it goes on and on. In an interview, Guibert said that, "Often when I write a book there is a writer behind me, as a ghost, a projected shadow on the text." For him that writer is Thomas Bernhard. For me that writer is Hervé Guibert. He is the ghost, the projected shadow, the echo.

At the end of *To the Friend* he buys enough doses of Digitaline in liquid form at a Roman pharmacy, a Chekhov's gun also setting up the suspense throughout his later books and film. "I'd have to choose between killing myself and writing a new book." Always the logic of suicide in his illness works, so much like his beloved Bernhard, who committed suicide on February 12, 1989, whose work Guibert is devouring as he writes this book. He deliberates throughout before picking up the prescription, as he worries having the bottle would make him act without thinking because of his despair, but perhaps it's better to act upon one's will, a real death. The staccato list of questions that follows that builds to a hysteric absurdity, pushing the Bernhardian digression into madness to a grotesque:

I'd add those seventy drops to a glass of water and drink them down, and then what would I do? Would I stretch out on the bed? Disconnect the phone? Play some music? What music? How long would it take before my heart stopped? What would I think about? Whom would I think about? Wouldn't I suddenly want to hear a voice? But whose? Wouldn't it be a voice I'd never have imagined wanting to hear at that moment? Would I want to masturbate until my blood stops dead, until my hand flies off my wrist? Have I just made a stupid mistake? Would I have been better off hanging myself? Matou says a radiator's enough, if you bend your knees. Wouldn't it have been better if I'd waited? Waited for that fake death from natural causes brought by the virus? And continued writing books, and drawing, and so on and so forth until I went mad?

TB

I remember now almost two years ago, the fall after my shingles, holding my breath for an echocardiogram, staring at the ceiling, counting tiles. I think of Thomas Bernhard, who Guibert punnily introduces only as "TB," accurately identifying the lifelong lung illness the Austrian novelist also suffered from, as the sensor slides in the clear goopy liquid in the middle of my chest, under my breasts, my side, the sliding hand under my hospital gown. I study the beautiful features of the technician as she takes videos of my insides and I think of Bernhard's fascination with his own death, a fascination that mirrors Guibert's, even from a young age. I finally was able to see a good cardiologist, for the severe chest pain of the February earlier where I was told again by an urgent care doctor that I was just run down, although there's an aberration on your EKG, see a cardiologist when you can. And it took a year to see one, to get new health insurance, proper although exorbitantly expensive health insurance for the year through the college. Stop nursing, the cardiologist, a sturdy New Yorker, tries to convince me again in her office afterwards, she is fine! She doesn't need it! I should spend more time with my nieces, she says, that will make me stress less, she starts to tell me about a place in midtown Manhattan where you dress up and have tea, I've stopped paying attention to her, after she said, perhaps it was a myocardial infarction, postpartum related, you should have seen me right away, yes, her teenagers now want nothing to do with her, the time really is gone before you know it.

WRITING THE BODY

"Here is what I did with my body one day . . ." writes Roland Barthes, quippily, in an entry in *Roland Barthes by Roland Barthes*. After a piece of his rib was removed while treating a collapsed lung, his Swiss doctors present it to him wrapped in gauze. He keeps this "rib chop" ("*la côtelette*"), in his desk drawer, along with such objects of the past as a childhood report card, a pink taffeta card case, and old keys. One day, he decides to fling "this fragment of myself," from his balcony, like a ceremonious scattering of ashes.

MANHOOD

That fall I read *Compassion Protocol* on a PDF on my phone, as it's out of print and I can't find a copy anywhere, standing over others on the commute. The Guibert narrator is recognized now on the bus heading to doctor appointments, in waiting rooms. He dedicates the follow-up to all those who wrote letters after the last book. The monotony of his appointments—what punctuates the inertia of his days. It is such a lonely book—his main encounters are with doctors, medical professionals are the only ones who touch him, including the young woman doctor he has a crush on for being kind to him, doctors and fans, the ones he hopes will flock to his gravesite in Elba. In many ways this book is full of more despair, saturated by this despair, and more beautiful. He is writing the book in front of us, against what time he has left, battling his crushing fatigue, it is impossible to run to catch the bus, he describes the slow way he must pull himself on, cling for support, how horrible to have to stand up when getting off. Here, the supposed new miracle drug that will allow him to write another book is DDI, part of a double-blind protocol, swiped off the bureau of a dead ballet dancer after he was cremated, presented to him by Jules stuffed into a plastic bag at the opening of the book. He hasn't been writing or reading, not until this one charged breathless entry that begins the book, an opening reminiscent of the full-body scan beginning Michel Leiris's *Manhood*, documenting an increasingly frail body, a body that can no longer crouch in the shower while the hot water runs over him, nor bathe sitting down, the agony lifting his arm to wash himself, he only wants to sleep, he sleeps all day in his armchair that is torture to get out of, sleep is his last full sensual pleasure now that he cannot swallow or fuck. He begins taking Prozac, and with the antidepressants surging through him, desire returns to begin this new book, even to begin the film. The drugs seize him like a possession, he takes on the energy of the young dead dancer. "It's the dead ballet dancer's DDI, with Prozac, writing the book for me . . ." Once the psych meds kick in, sleep becomes "voluptuous" again. "I was alive again. I was writing again. I was horny again. Soon, perhaps I would fuck again." I think about that moment in the introduction to *Touching Feeling* when Eve Sedgwick, suffering from metastatic breast cancer, apologizes for being such a bad Foucauldian because there's no fucking in her book. And yet there's an erotic charge to Guibert's language in *Compassion Protocol*, to the desire and inability to write throughout, the deferred fuck is writing. It's almost holy in its abjectness.

REVULSION

Almost all of the fucking described in the first book is remembered in the past tense, the before period, as the narrator attempts to piece together not only the moment of contagion but his and Jules' "semi-oblivion" in relation to the plague for most of the decade. He writes in his diary in 1981 after watching Jules fuck a "little blond curly-haired masseur" who was covered in scabs, who they picked up in a bathhouse as a present for their shared birthday, "Yet at the same time, we were all catching the disease from one another's bodies. We would have caught leprosy, if we could have." Very different from the "mutual massacre" birthday celebration in Lisbon once they know, they are both raw with suffering, especially Jules, who is completely devastated, making physical closeness unbearable. In the novel Jules is described as needy and insatiable, and his lover must pity-fuck him after the now-official certainty of their diagnosis, even though they found it difficult now that they knew, the virus a "repellent specter," even though the only risk was a "reciprocal recontamination." His wife Berthe had also developed a revulsion towards his body once learning, for both of Jules's lovers like their vision becoming unblinkered after eating from the tree of knowledge. "And we both knew that Jules couldn't live and wouldn't survive unless he felt desired." There is the beautifully sad scene of Jules confessing that he is going blind, a sign of AIDS, a white layer coating his cornea—the metatextual layers of this, as Thierry Journo directed a center for the blind, this is how they met, as Guibert was a tutor there and it served as the setting of his novel *Blindsight*—and so the narrator goes about the rituals of sex play, going through the motions of hurting him, clamping his nipples, getting him to moan, to kneel at his feet. As the narrator comes Jules gives him the "unbearable" gaze that he worries he has at the beginning of the book, the naked almost blind gaze of being close to death, like Rilke describes in his elegies.

This attempt at fucking struck me right away as unspeakably sad: I felt as though Jules and I had gotten lost between our lives and our deaths, that this no-man's-land, ordinarily and necessarily rather nebulous, had suddenly become atrociously clear, that we are taking our places, through this physical coupling, in a macabre tableau of two sodomitical skeletons. Jammed all the way up my ass, deep in the flesh around my pelvic arch, Jules made me come as he gazed into my eyes. It was an unbearable look, too sublime, too wrenching, both eternal and threatened by eternity. I caught the sob in my throat by making it sound like a sigh of relief.

Only a couple pages later Guibert is worrying over the implications of continuing to have sex with the character he calls The Poet with whom he has not seemingly disclosed his status, a teenage boy (albeit with a child's face and adolescent body, so age is uncertain) described as a libertine, whose mother has already taken him to get tested earlier, assuming his relationship with the narrator and Jules was physical, although, as Guibert writes, he had always been careful, distinguishing himself seemingly from Muzil's high-risk endeavors, "even when he'd begged me to treat him like a slut, and when I'd handed him over to Jules, whom I used as the dildo I didn't care to be." Although he always put new condoms on Jules, he worries that they've become "godless, lawless murderers," wondering if one can tell by the smell of the sweat emanating from their bodies, as if describing the scene of a crime, as (always) channeled through Genet. But it's ambivalent whether this anxiety is because of legal ramifications, noting at the beginning of the section that prosecutions are beginning to happen with casual sex partners knowingly transmitting the virus, or whether it's out of true ethical concerns. He does, earlier in the work, translate Muzil's delighted description of the barebacking at the San Francisco bathhouse, in a spirit of, I think, nonjudgment. And what am I to think of the ways Guibert writes his relationship to his partner's children, both in the journals and here? He describes his love for them as having replaced sex for him, along with the collection of objects, the accumulation of his drawings, and his writing here.

> I think the pleasures these children give me are greater than the ones of the flesh, of other attractive and satisfying flesh, which I renounce for the moment out of lassitude, preferring to accumulate new objects and drawings around me, like a pharaoh preparing the furnishings of his tomb, with his own image multiplied over and over to mark the entrance, or on the contrary to obscure it with detours, lies, and simulacra.

The autoportrait as one's image multiplied at the opening of a tomb, as if to hope for immortality. This is yet another way Guibert gives us to read the book, like a game he is playing, a game of seeming truth-telling that's obscured with "detours, lies, simulacra." I think The Poet is Vincent, the object of Guibert's infatuation, whose death he imagines in his chronicle *Crazy for Vincent*, who was fifteen when Guibert met him in 1982. In *Compassion Protocol*, he's just Vincent. I don't know why it's important to me, to decode this play with names across the books. And here, The Poet is described as a fuck puppet or toy, an unpaid trick and trainwreck to hand around to their group of pervy older male friends, including a past New Year's party with the character of the priest, who dies of undisclosed AIDS, and also, that he's sad to learn that he doesn't have AIDS. I can say I both admire Guibert's intensity of his obsession as it translates to literature, but find almost none of the sex or the living of his glory days hot. I'm not sure if I'm supposed to. I am reminded of Moyra Davey getting turned off by all the acts of transgression in Genet in her *Burn the Diaries*, whose writing she is imbibing initially with such dedication, cutting up his complete works and reading them on the subway, a total immersion that seeps into her dreams, and moving instead to reading Violette Leduc. Can't I, like Moyra Davey writes of *Funeral Rites*, both love and hate this book? Perhaps I should make "good" and "bad" columns in my notebook like she describes. I remember rereading Plato's *Symposium* years back and realizing it read like a drunken orgy that was only fun for the white older men, served by slaves. Here too was the origin for Foucault's utopia of the eros of male homo relationships. Socrates, let's admit it, was a creep.

TOP/BOTTOM

In the introduction to the tape journals, David Velasco writes that David Wojnarowicz wrote with the voice of a bottom, "a searching, moral voice, a voice that says, 'Use me if you've been used and enjoy being used because I've been used and enjoyed it too'"— and he does write from the point of view of the former teenage hustler, who's been used and traumatized, who still finds tendernesses and solidarities and pleasure with johns and strangers, as well as from the formless paternal friendships that Foucault writes to. It's not for me to moralize any position among consensual adults, including roleplay with domination and submission or the politics of the bathhouse before the exact way AIDS was transmitted was known, or even during the height of AIDS. But I also don't know whether Guibert writes as a top or a bottom.

FIBROSCOPY

Once Guibert documents his medical torments, his subject-position changes. He is now at the mercy of his doctors and what they do to him. In *Compassion Protocol*, a devastating scenario of a fibroscopy with a sadistic doctor, a doctor who sees him as "nothing more than just another infected little faggot, who was going to kick the bucket in any case, and who was wasting his time." Guibert narrates the tube going down his throat, he looks upon his own body from the top of the ceiling, in order to endure the trauma of this procedure, where he is "alone on the paper-sheeted table in the huge empty room." When he gets home he can only open up his journal and write one word: "Fibroscopy." "I had become incapable of recounting my experience," he writes.

The will it takes to write a page when sick. The absolute need to write because it feels utterly futile, and private, and necessary. To retain some humanity. The ephemerality and urgency of an individual consciousness, recording what it's like to be a body in time and space. Throughout his portrait of Muzil as well as his own self-documentation, Guibert reenacts Foucault's theories of the medical gaze, what happens to the subject's identity once he becomes a patient, how heroic it is to attempt to reclaim the subject in an increasingly bureaucratized and medicalized body:

> Muzil spent a morning in the hospital having tests done, and told me he'd forgotten how completely the body loses all identity once it's delivered into medical hands, becoming just a package of helpless flesh, trundled around here and there, hardly even a number on a slip of paper . . .

ER

Always a health crisis precipitates my looping return to the Guibert study, my own experiences of the alienating clinical gaze, which can't seem to look back at me as though I'm fully human. It was right before the last Easter when I had another heart episode and wound up in the ER. Sitting in a hot window-less basement room teaching, constricted by control-top tights I have no idea why I chose to wear, I managed to get myself home, vomited, semi-passed out on the floor, and became aware of my body pulsating and burning—down my back, down one arm, especially my chest. I then panicked that I was dying, that I was having a heart attack, then made the incredibly stupid decision to have John drive me to a Brooklyn ER as opposed to urgent care. I didn't know until after that everyone says not to go to the emergency room in New York City, unless you are actually dying, unless you are bleeding from the head or have lost an essential limb, because all you will do is wait, wait the entire night, and possibly catch another disease. John stayed in the car with Leo asleep in the backseat. We didn't know who to ask to take her so he could go with me, but what would be the point, one is always alone in such abject situations, company is impossible, what would he do, pull a Shirley MacLaine for my Debra Winger, as I once did for my mother as she waited in one of the ER stalls, shivering, please, please, can my mother be seen now? But my mother was dying, she was actually dying, I was merely experiencing the blip of my mortality, a blip of the mysterious T waves that keep on flipping since giving birth. Even though I was not a stranger to ERs—although they were suburban ERs and in the past—that night is the closest I have ever felt to existing in purgatory, there was no way to leave, there was no way out, not unless they chose to release me. They wouldn't let me leave, not once I had been admitted. First I waited on a hard chair in the waiting room, folded over my big bag, I had left the house without a bra, wearing only a large sweater and baggy jeans. From the waiting room, I was moved through the plastic curtains to where I would sit for hours in a chair wedged between two stretchers, my back hitting the hard desk of the nurse's station. Since I could still walk I needed to sit on a chair, there were no beds available, there wouldn't be any beds available all night, on the right of me an ancient woman in the violent throes of dementia, muttering and barely conscious, her dry and bony foot, its long yellowed nails, almost touching me, a cast on the other foot. I jumped up when the orderlies almost banged her foot against me as they positioned her next to me. On my left an addict, curled up, cradling a bottle of yellow liquid on the stretcher that looked like urine, his jangly naked thigh exposed, he had also injured his foot and kept on complaining he needed more painkillers, he was told they needed a clean urine sample to get more drugs, he kept on watching cartoons on his phone, lunging back, his head near my knee, abutting the nurse's station. We were in the way, the hallway, but no one saw me when they passed by, I wasn't actually there at all. Besides the guy next to me it was almost entirely a geriatric ward, some with adult sons and daughters who held their hands or sat with them, dazed and silent, or on their phones and passing time, accustomed to this ordeal, others alone, like my lady next to me, her moan deep and low and constant, registering she was still conscious. All of the moaning and screaming was what unsettled me, I wanted to run away, kept on asking if I could leave, no one could hear or listen to me. The alarm kept on going off for the elderly man directly across from me whose son had just left, I think related to his blood pressure. I began to try to wave down the nurse for him. I read Clutch's book and took notes on my phone. After hours of waiting, I was finally led into various semi-private rooms to get a chest X-ray, then yet another EKG, by arrogant young men, where I took off my sweater, exposing my sagging flat breasts, my nakedness unremarkable among all the concave bare chests around me, the bruises of their IVs. It wasn't that I was disassociating exactly—more that I was not presently alive but instead living in a fuzzy memory of last being an uncomfortable unclothed body in a medical context, not a person, just a body. I couldn't leave until they took urine from me, then a blood sample, which took forever. The bathroom was filthy, I kicked open the door gingerly rather than turn the handle, ran the faucet with my elbows, there was no soap next to the sink. The contrast of the poshness of my uptown cardiologist's office the next day. Her hair looked blonder since September. I still felt the sticky soreness of my ripped-off bandages, the cheap hospital bandages that tear at your skin, the various veins poked at before they could find one that wouldn't collapse, I was severely dehydrated, I wasn't drinking any water while waiting there. What kind of books do you write again? Sounds serious. Her kids are now in college, going to NYU and Columbia for free. They turn fourteen, and they want nothing to do with you, it'll break your heart, enjoy your time while you can, she says again, repeating herself. She doesn't seem especially concerned about the chest pain, how it comes and goes, or if she is, she doesn't show it. Just try to stress less, okay? You're going to drop dead if you don't, is that what you want, to drop dead?

LOVE STORIES

What do you write, a nurse asks the narrator as she ties the band around his arm. Thrillers? No, love stories. She laughs. I don't believe you, you're too young to write love stories. The final passages of the novel become almost giddy again, filled with gossip and tenderness as the narrator gets blood work regularly at the Spallanzani Clinic in Rome, he delights in the drama, the camaraderie between the nuns and the infected junkies, despite the anonymity of these encounters, "relishing the moments of sweet humanity that never failed to spring from the harshest cruelty."

ALICE AND EVE

In *Compassion Protocol*, Jules and the narrator discuss Robert Mapplethorpe's self-portrait, taken in New York in 1988, how sculpted his face is from illness, the head looks like it's floating in space because of the black turtleneck he wears, the hand in the foreground gripping a walking stick with a tiny skeleton head at the top, the face of death. Mapplethorpe was to die one year after this photograph was taken of AIDS-related illness. It's a self-portrait but the shot was taken by his younger brother, just like, in the novel, Jules wants to be the one to photograph his lover's skeletal frame. Mapplethorpe had photographed an elderly Alice Neel years earlier in 1984, mouth open, eyes closed, how the light hits her crepey spotted skin, its translucence, the white wisp of her hair like a halo. Neel confided to him she was dying of colon cancer. She died only one week later. It's incredibly intimate, this photograph, her confession, the vulnerability of being so near death, the openness of her mouth. It's like we are watching her asleep faintly snoring. Like how Guibert in *Compassion Protocol* describes the erotics of the swollen balloon of his elderly aunt's naked body underneath her robe. He now has aged like her, they have the same life expectancy, like the kindredness of Mapplethorpe and Neel. I keep on switching back and forth between this Mapplethorpe photograph of Alice Neel and the photograph of the painter when she is younger, sitting cross-legged in front of her paintings, slouched over, that intense stare, her glossy brunette hair. Still the same shape of the face, it's the same face. Even with a dying Mapplethorpe, it's the same face, hair thinning, the same moody expression, except steelier. I keep on switching back and forth between self-portraits of Guibert and then Mapplethorpe, these two dreamily gorgeous photographers aged half a lifetime in just years, because of the incredible cruelty of this disease. We reproduce and so remember the young portraits more often partially because the ones of their frailty are unspeakably sad. The elegiac end of Eve Sedgwick's essay on paranoid and reparative reading—how AIDS disrupted the natural lineage of the younger generation replacing the old. She also includes within this the intellectuals she knows who are dying of cancer and other illnesses without health insurance, her own limited life expectancy because of her metastasized cancer.

AUTOPORTRAIT

Sometime in the winter of 2019, I have no time to work on the Guibert book, but I go by Callicoon Fine Arts on the Lower East Side to another show of fifteen of his black-and-white photographs of friends and lovers. Penis! my daughter says delightedly, pointing at a joyously masturbating Thierry. I focus on one self-portrait I've never seen, with its cheeky framing a quintessential Guibert. Posing in a T-shirt, naked from the waist down except for socks, in the bathroom, a towel on the floor, in front of a mirror. That extravagantly beautiful face, the crown of cherub curls. The shock of Guibert's beautiful face. The contrast: he is unafraid to be ugly in his writing voice. How Muzil mourned his young protégé cutting off his curls when he turned 30, this is three months before his mentor's death, his new sterner face, the face (he notes) he will have at his death. The older philosopher had just seen his mentee on TV, at the Césars, when he still had his curly mop. The fear of aging throughout all of Guibert's writing, and yet despite never aging past thirty-six, how sped-up the aging process of his illness. How vain Guibert is in the diaries, even in his twenties worried about his thinning hair. He largely stopped taking self-portraits when he was no longer beautiful. There are just the first-person books that remain. There is the much-reproduced photograph of him lying down, hair shorn. Autoportait, 1989. Already diagnosed, under treatment. He is more severe, still beautiful. (When he sees a friend at dinner, the friend remarks how he is still so good-looking.) Is this one of his last autoportraits? Like Dürer, who stopped his handsome self-portraits once in middle age (the devastation of Dürer's portrait of his dying mother, the agony of her wizened face). Throughout the novel he refuses to look in the faces of the men he sees in the waiting rooms, these wretches who stare at each other, how youthful and beautiful they look at first, contrast to the "death's head" they see when looking in the mirror. The melting of his face to the "cadaverous" by the end, as his weight drops. While getting blood work in one of the flash moments at the end, in Rome, he looks in the mirror and finally sees himself again as extravagantly handsome, despite viewing himself as a skeleton throughout, he has accepted his face, he can love himself again, is that, he wonders, the height or the renunciation of his narcissism.

WHY DID YOU INVITE HER?

That summer I reread the Sedgwick essay on paranoid and repar-ative reading—as Sofia references it when I worry to her I'm not cosmopolitan enough or queer enough to write about Guibert, that I would never have been included in Foucault's circle. I am a mom on a couch! And yet it soothes me to remember that Sedgwick wrote mainly of a community of gay men. When she argues that the depressive position is one of repair and love. Of course you're sensitive about charges of writing about him while not being like him, or not being radical enough—in this world of paranoia, you would have to be very ignorant, or else some kind of mystic being, not to be worried about that! Sofia writes. For me the project is valuable precisely because it's not in line with our paranoid ethos, because it doesn't privilege identity and boundaries and protecting the self from exposure above all else. Which means you can look at different things—and be indulgent and ridiculous! Because I don't share his position, Sofia writes me, maybe I can offer another sort of writing.

DISAPPEARANCE

Earlier this summer I wrote a story, "Disappearance," inspired by *To the Friend Who Did Not Save My Life*, about a friend who I once knew online, where I wondered about whether I have betrayed my friend by writing about her. Writing this story about my friend didn't satisfy my desire to write a study of Hervé Guibert's novel. It didn't satisfy me philosophically and, probably most importantly, it didn't satisfy the contract I had signed to write a study of Hervé Guibert's novel. So I must begin again, when I only have months left to write it.

THE LAST DAYS OF MUZIL

The question at the center of *To the Friend Who Did Not Save My Life*: Was it a betrayal to write about his friend in his most private moments—the moment of his disintegration and death? Guibert writes an extended portrait of his friend's last days, like the Jacques-Louis David painting *The Death of Socrates*: The Last Days of Muzil. In the hospital room, the Guibert narrator is disturbed by Muzil's naked muscled torso, like Socrates's in the painting. A young companion gives Socrates the chalice of hemlock, looking away either in shame or already in mourning. How vulnerable Muzil appears, in the hospital room smelling of fried fish, without his trademark glasses, with that tender detail of the bit of dried blood on the back of his head from the fall that landed him in the hospital, with his exhaustion and wrack-ing cough, with his fright at an upcoming spinal tap. The Muzil sections overdetermined the book for contemporary French readers and resulted in the scandal that would make the book famous. There was a trial in the media, first in the papers, who were already vulturous for details of Michel Foucault's death, and then Guibert himself appearing on the talk show *Apostrophes*, on March 16, 1990. I watch the interview on YouTube. My student Philo, a native of Paris, has translated it for me, although I can make out phrases and also tone, which feels scolding or accu-satory on the part of the interviewer, Bernard Pivot, stern and defensive on the part of Guibert. Guibert is obviously extremely sick. His blazer is huge on him, the floppy collar of his bright blue shirt. His huge head covered barely by thinning hair (that once-beautiful hair, still the sandy color). Those rimmed eyes. He speaks at first of the premonitory atmosphere of AIDS, how he wished not to have it follow him. The interviewer asks him (this is all so Pontius Pilate, this circling around cruelty and ethics and privacy): "There is the recurring question: do you have the right to narrate the agony and the death of Michel Foucault who was a friend of yours?" He doesn't know, he says. But does this death belong to anyone? he then answers. All he knows is that he was put on trial in the papers by those who hadn't read the book, who had already formed their own opinions as to his betrayal.

CANDY DARLING ON HER DEATHBED

I keep on going back to Guibert saying that it felt more like a betrayal when he photographed his friends than when he wrote about them. But his writing of Foucault disintegrating on his deathbed is not unlike a form of photography. Isn't this what David Wojnarowicz does so elegiacally on film and in his series of 23 photographs of his love and mentor Peter Hujar, recorded moments after his death, the almost religious panning of his hands and his feet? And what Peter Hujar did in his portraits of Candy Darling in her hospital bed and others? Although Hujar still keeps Candy Darling beautiful, there is nothing of death to the photograph, she arranges herself, the folds of her hospital sheets like a gown. The rawness of Guibert's portrait in prose of his friend's frailty in conflict with the polish of Foucault's body, head, books. Foucault's desire to have only the monuments exist, "the well-polished bare bones."

I compare the translated transcript of the talk show to his confession in the novel itself. He never says this isn't a betrayal, only that he feels the desire to write these scenes of a hospital room, a premonition of his future. In the novel he documents the steps taken for the privacy of this famous patient, his name obscured and falsified from the paper trail, screening visitors out of the worry "some vulture" would take a picture of him. Protecting these scenes from future biographers, from the media. His friend is there by his side, holding his hand, kissing his hand, and then documenting going home and washing his lips out of shame and revulsion, a parallel scene to washing his lips when he is kissed in Mexico on the dancefloor. The shame of writing in the book of washing his lips, the need to write or exorcise this shame and fear. "It is awful to write this," the interviewer says of that scene. "Yes it's awful but it's the truth," Guibert replies. Truth has its cruelty and its delicacy, its delicacy and barbarism, as Guibert has written of Sade. For he also writes a scene of the narrator and Muzil holding hands, the way they would when on Muzil's white couch, after having supper in his kitchen. Every time he came home from the hospital, he writes reports in his journal. "I was writing intolerable things. I think I was doing this in order to forget those things because when I write, all of what I write, once it is written, it is forgotten." To write so as to forget, to cleanse oneself, not to remember. Still when he writes this report in the novel five years later, he cannot consult his journal, it is too much to go back. He knows that Foucault would have felt betrayed, that this was in fact a betrayal. "I knew that Muzil would have been so hurt if he'd known I was writing reports of everything like a spy, like an adversary, all these degrading little things, in my diary." So what gives him the right to this? we ask when reading this. Guibert asks himself. The interviewer, Bernard Pivot, asks him also. It is his shame he is writing about, his degradation. How he washes the kiss away, that gesture, how he must get out his diary and write, another gesture.

THE YEAR WITHOUT NAMES

The closeting and taboo of writing about this illness Guibert lays bare. To write the shame, the fear, the specter of death circling his friend group. For it is really his agony he is forecasting, his own imagined illness and death. What is it to witness such a terrible death? It was his to witness. It was his then to write. The story is of a friendship, the time period the length of the incubation of the mysterious illness that he suspects he has carried along with him all of this time, like a secret narrative. The slow growth of friendship mirrors the slow growth of the disease. First he witnesses his mentor's death and then he pays witness to his own. An AIDS diagnosis at this time, especially in French bourgeois society, was supposed to be private and anonymous, and throughout Guibert refers to the discretion and confidentiality of personal physicians. When Muzil dies, his conservative sister wishes for his cause of death to be struck from the registrar: "The sister had demanded that they cross this out, that they blacken it completely, or scratch it out if they had to, or even better, tear out the page and redo it, for while these records are of course confidential, still, you never know, perhaps in ten or twenty years some muckracking biographer will come and Xerox the entry, or X-ray the impression still faintly legible on the page." No one claimed to know that Muzil had AIDS, everyone is supposed to remain cheerful around him, but there was a veil over the entire proceedings—they knew but they didn't want to disclose, because the disclosure was seen as impure. AIDS was clouded in secrecy and privacy because of the aura of shame surrounding it, because it was, as Sontag writes in *AIDS and Its Metaphors*, a plague, which was seen as moral punishment, a disgrace. The Institut Alfred-Fournier, where Guibert goes for blood work in Paris, was originally a syphilis hospital, and Sontag contextualizes the sense of contagion and repulsion attached to AIDS as closest to the diagnosis of syphilis, as "punishment for a person's transgression." A polluting person is always wrong, Sontag cites Mary Douglas in her analysis on concepts of pollution and taboo. Guibert is seen as wrong, because AIDS was seen as a horrible pollution. And so was gossip about it. This is an impure, outing, bitchy book, whose shock around its apparent transgressions (outing, gossiping, but also contracting AIDS in the first place) reveals intense moral hypocrisy and puritanism. More than anything, his soul of indiscretion is counter to polite bourgeois French society. The question throughout these pages—how much did Foucault know about his diagnosis, and what did his doctors and secretary keep from him, a practice of cloistering information from the patient that Foucault himself wrote about? This can be read as crossing a boundary—outing his yearly sojourns to the San Francisco bathhouses despite having some knowledge of how AIDS was communicated, even celebrating the radical intimacy and openness taking place there, that the danger of the disease has created "new complicities, new tenderness, new solidarities," which seems to suggest that even though statuses weren't disclosed, everyone was operating with the knowledge that they could transmit AIDS to one other. A double layer to this betrayal—Foucault's own obsession with privacy (a "closet queen," as Guibert says of him in an interview.) Throughout this continuum of being tested in the novel, Guibert relies, as others did, on a system of pseudonyms, on the anonymity of the disease, while having moments of revelation that a secret is not going to protect him from the inevitable. The nurse "calling out the names written there, and then they called out mine, but there's a stage in this sickness when keeping it secret just doesn't matter anymore, it even becomes hateful and burdensome." When he is supposed to be getting the blood work that hangs over the narrative of most of the book, his doctor realizes it's been a year since he's been seeing him, saying something about how quickly time flies. "Later I wondered if he'd said that intentionally to remind me that my days were now numbered, that I shouldn't waste them writing under or about another name than my own." Perhaps he can write this because he knows he is dying. That's why there's no betrayal. He is already a ghost. He cannot hide his illness from his friends or his readers as his mentor did, he cannot keep it from haunting his friendships. The book is also a confession. "Like Muzil, I would have liked to have had the strength, the insane pride, as well as the generosity, to tell no one, allowing friendships to live as lightly as air, carefree and eternal." A premonition: The autoportrait taken in 1986 at rue du Moulin-Vert. The author on a massage bed with white covers drawn up at the center of a living room, like a staged morgue, his head peeking out. Even before he was to find out the results of his blood work, "I felt death approaching in the mirror, gazing back at me from my own reflection . . ."

NAUSEA

How time freezes and then speeds up. The winter of 2020, once my classes begin, I cannot work anymore on the Guibert study. I do not have the time anymore, and also I am overwhelmed by the extreme labor of my nausea, which I attempt to mitigate with all of the recommended remedies—forcing a hard-boiled egg first thing in the morning, ginger candy, the sweaty pinch of my acupressure wristbands. A prescription allows me a faint swell of appetite, enough to eat a single Shake Shack burger, in the car when John drives me the hour or two to my classes, which I then struggle to keep down. On my days off I nap on and off all day. I try to read Virginia Woolf on illness. The desire to be productive when ill—in this other space. The space of confinement as a site of knowledge, of productiveness, despite cramped and limited time, the foreclosure of a fragile body. How one can see in a different way.

THE PLAGUE

And then, the ambiance of paranoia of the spring eerily echoes the book I've been residing in. It crept in at first as a murmur of worries and all of a sudden it was everywhere—the fever pitch of anxiety about another mysterious illness wreaking havoc on the immune system. No one can get tested—there are no tests anywhere. The only ones who get tested are celebrities who then post unbearably earnest videos about their recovery. More than a year's wait for a vaccine, longer, most likely. The vaccine a Godot that never comes in Guibert's book, though he is promised privileged access because of his social circle, his good looks, his celebrity status. I can't manage to reread the Guibert novel during this time. I sit on the couch and reread Sontag's *Illness as Metaphor*. In her follow-up, on AIDS, looking back at the previous book, she writes that she wished to write a book that would "calm the imagination, not incite it." How counter her logic is to Guibert's (inflamed) first-person work, which draws from the hyperbolic rhetoric of apocalypse as well as the military metaphor that she critiques. The way he depicts the rumors about AIDS mirrors the "classic script for plague" Sontag writes about. Its imagined foreignness—Muzil musing that it must have come from monkeys in Africa, the theories that it was transmitted from animals, the connection between the other and animality. The president and others call this the Chinese flu, as it's rumored to have originated in the wet markets in Wuhan, China, and so there's an outbreak of violence and racial hatred against Asian Americans, but it also comes to New York from Italy. Strangely there's also a reference to the Chinese flu throughout *To the Friend*—when on a crushed Métro the narrator breathes through his nose, not wanting to catch it, it's what Berthe and the children actually are suffering from, which they survive. There is also the acupuncture scene with the fat doctor with the Chinese name and his dirty instruments—more fear of contagion.

The eerie parallels of the novel to now. The sci-fi feeling of isolation in Rome, where Guibert exiles himself—with Rome now, the vacant streets, the eeriness of the emptied-out Spanish Steps. In two weeks New York is supposed to be where Italy is now. The horror stories of doctors having to choose who gets to live or die. New York City is not prepared, there are not enough beds or ventilators, everything is exhausted and overrun already. In the waiting room for an ultrasound I try to read my shabby paperback of Camus's *The Plague*—I stop after a few pages, having lost my appetite at all the bloody rats. To go to this appointment, I wear medical gloves and one of a few masks that we find, John's stash from his studio. We drive past the tented triage station set outside Mount Sinai West, the stretchers on the street, ambulances crowding in. Right when I enter the second trimester, in the middle of March, New York City completely shuts down. The governor orders a shelter in place without calling it that. All last week on the front page of *The New York Times*, the plummeting stocks sit on top of the dead, which sickens me. The death rate is rising here—it's now worse than Wuhan. The constant whine of the ambulance sirens on our street. My daughter's preschool closes. I miss my friends she wails to us every night. When she falls asleep, she wakes up cold and covered in urine. The same ritual—we sleepily take her to the bath, run the water, I sponge her off, hug her cold wet body, towel her dry, hold her while she weeps as John runs down the wet bedding. I cancel my amniocentesis, despite being at an advanced age for birth defects, an agonizing decision, in order to not have to go to the medical center more than necessary. I weigh percentages versus other percentages against our own panic. So much is still unknown—the mortality rate, whether the virus mostly affects the elderly or immunocompromised. The obits of all of these queer men, culture workers in their sixties and seventies, who survived AIDS, now dying of coronavirus. We have stopped leaving the house—it's been cold and rainy. The CDC is now advising people to wear masks—we try to figure out how to order or make cloth masks. Dr. Fauci is on American television again. The uncanny doubling and return of language that those who were adults and at risk during the height of the AIDS crisis know so well. Secret vaccine trials. Risk management. Rumors of contagion. Viral load. Shedding of the virus. We learn that the virus is "simply a piece of bad news wrapped up in protein." A virus hijacks cells to replicate and spread when it finds a cell, it injects a shard of RNA that contains the coronavirus genome. The paranoia of the internet. Various theories. Everyone is now an epidemiologist. There's nothing else to read or think about. It is now gloomy and raining outside. I wonder if my pneumonia in November and December was actually somehow this virus. Mirroring the speculative latency Guibert traces of his illness—hypochondriac or the breakdown of his immune system? Worried that I woke up with pain in my right eye, as a very small percentage of cases report conjunctivitis, but there's no red or gunk so far. The secondary infections that are the locus of Guibert's hypervigilance, once he knows he is positive—like the swollen gland he obsessively fingers, finally getting a prescription at a futuristic pharmacy in Vatican City like out of a Kubrick film.

LIST

At least we are lucky. We are not sick. We can teach our classes at home. We are told this throughout, the privilege and moral responsibility of staying home. What an experiment for a social body. On the flip side, in the midst of a pandemic, we are expected to teach at home, learn this new technology overnight, without our three-year-old in preschool or with the help of childcare, still no sick or parenting leave for adjuncts. This is a pandemic—is it a plague according to Sontag's definition, i.e., a moral panic? The judgment online of who is going out, who is fleeing the city. Who is not staying six feet away. Who is going to parks and beaches, although later outside will be deemed relatively safe. We cast judgment on those who leave the city. We are not wealthy enough to leave for a second vacation home upstate or in the Hamptons. We have no retreat. We are sticking it out here. Every day we ask each other—should we leave? But where would we go? Not to elderly parents in the Midwest, the horror anyway of their small-minded Catholicism. (Guibert's fervent desire in the novel not to die in the spotlight of the parental eye.) Or to rural towns with only one ventilator. There are first-person reports now of healthy people in their thirties and forties getting deathly ill—a freak-out of the immune system—the repetition of the testimonials, the inability to smell or taste, the body aches, the fever and the sweats, the inability to breathe, the unbearable fatigue. We stay awake at night, scrolling, living in a protective bubble of our own dread. Every writer with a byline publishes a coronavirus diary, even if they are never sick, especially then, just narrating the atmosphere, the same anecdotes, same language. Attempting sense out of the logic of plague panic—the run on toilet paper, disinfecting wipes, hand sanitizer, flour, active dried yeast, diapers. I spend all day trying to score far-too-expensive small spritzers of an organic hand sanitizer with the right percentage of ethyl alcohol made in rural Pennsylvania. Everything is sold out at our local bodegas and stores, we poke our head in and ask if more hand sanitizers and cleaners have been delivered, scurry out. We begin getting our groceries delivered, which we disinfect with our last Lysol wipes. We spend far too much on these groceries, like the only sensual pleasures afforded to us now. Several types of berries, which I co eats full packages of in the morning, having been frozen on a truck most likely for weeks, picked by migrant workers, we convince ourselves this isn't so because they are labeled organic. Smushy bags of frozen pineapple and cold wet bunches of lacinato kale for green smoothies, which I refuse, I refuse the moral superiority of the green smoothie urged on me by John and the midwives. Cartons of cage-free eggs—all I want to eat are eggs, John makes poached eggs, eggs over easy; broccoli omelets with shallots, three scrambled eggs with cheese for my breakfast, so many types of cheese—provolone, three cheddars, the sliced yellow cheddar for sandwiches, the medium sharp block from Wisconsin, yellow and familiar, and the aged from Vermont, white and crumbly; the hard cheeses, wedges of parmesan and pecorino romano, fresh mozzarella floating peacefully in its plastic home, John is trying his hand at pizzas, so much cheese in the broken plastic drawer in the refrigerator kept together with duct tape. We stuff the fridge so full with these groceries we have no idea what we bought, it seems everything expires. The right brand of oat milk, full-fat dairy milk. Old-fashioned rolled oats. The good type of corn tortillas even though we already have several packages. Organic turkey bacon. Artisanal Brooklyn smoked nova lox. Two containers of plain organic full-fat Australian Greek-style yogurt which we eat with the berries. Unsalted Irish butter. Plastic containers of butterhead lettuce, grown on a hydroponic rooftop farm somewhere in Brooklyn, we forget to use them and they stack up expired, condensation on each lid, containers we either open and dump and then recycle or, nothing mattering anymore, throw entirely away. Organic peasant bread that goes stale immediately and blooms into mold three days later. Small fortunes in organic peanut butter and organic almond butter. Multigrain waffle mix. Grade A maple syrup. We become popsicle parents—boxes of organic popsicles and containers of ice cream for Leo, as if the sheer varieties of frozen sweets could help her forget that we're not letting her see her friends. Three-year-olds without their shirts on attempt video chats while sitting in front of their iPads or parents' computers while eating expensive out-of-season watermelon or popsicles— if one of them is having a snack, the other one wants an equivalent snack—conversations that end in tears or the singing of songs from *Frozen*, a movie my daughter finds too scary. Already-ripe avocadoes that come in plastic container armor, the tomatoes that don't taste like tomatoes, the varieties of fruit, we are now grateful for the protection of the plastic, there is so much

waste, the green bananas shrouded in foam wrap that we immediately throw out. We order off Amazon what we could get down
the street, the plastic containers of prenatal gummies, the vita-
mins with iron make me more nauseous. Leo plays in the over-
sized boxes, creating tunnels or robot costumes, until they are
broken down and bound for the recycling trucks. We re-up our
medium-roasted nongenetically modified coffee subscriptions
which arrive in boxes thrown on our porch. We stay inside bak-
ing muffins and attempting to roast chickens on sheet pans following the online cooking craze and soaking heirloom beans
delivered by people without a safety net of sick pay or health
insurance. The perversity and cruelty of all of this. The pandemic
exposes the social inequity of our capitalist hellscape, we stay
inside attempting to make hobbies out of the unending mainte-
nance labor while others are still commuting to work exposed,
without protective gear. We stay up to try to reserve a slot to get
groceries delivered, new slots which becomes available online at
midnight, the groceries then coming in the massive truck parked
on our street, we jump when the bell is rung, just leave the bags
on the porch, like the worker delivering the boxes is somehow
going to infect us when they are the ones most at risk from us, we
assuage ourselves we gave a nice tip, if we can't get one of the
weekly slots we pay for someone to go to the grocery store that
day and shop for us, agree to replacements over text that are further away from what we wanted, hopeful we can score toilet
paper. People here clap condescendingly at 7 p.m. every night for
the essential workers delivering them their essential goods and
hospital workers. I don't clap, I feel gross at this hero language,
everyone should be able to stay at home unless they have sick
leave, hazard pay, and adequate protective equipment, there's a
man on his fourth-floor balcony across the street who blows his
shofar like an elephant, someone always sets off their car alarm,

on some days it feels less thankful and more like a form of catharsis that lasts for minutes, rattling at our claustrophobia, a roar of hooting and clapping, cars honking as they race down the street. John meets our twice-a-month housekeeper on the street when she is coming to clean and gives her money for the next two months—we keep on sending her the money all summer although we are often late as we don't want to go to the post office. She tells us everyone is canceling and nobody's paying her. Of course, I am supposed to be as productive teaching as ever. Yesterday weeping, reeling over an email from the dean at the college, they *hoped* to honor the contracts of guest faculty but have to wait until enrollment in the summer. Same response from the university. My health insurance is set to expire then the week I am supposed to give birth—where would we live, how would we pay rent? Half the world ordered to stay home. Ten million have applied for unemployment. How strange, if this keeps up, I will be able to teach at home, if I am still offered classes, I might get something resembling maternity leave, not officially of course, working but working from home, forgoing the impossible commute with a newborn.

CITIZEN OF THE NIGHT

There's a strange feeling of isolation now like when I had a newborn—the sense of no time, being inside, constantly worrying about death, my death, the death of those around me. It's Sontag's time of illness, of being a citizen of the night. A dread planet. My belly is hard now—not that anyone can see it. I haven't taken one photo of my body. She's swimming and swimming inside me—the pulsating is some sort of affect. I need to write this study before I give birth in August. Or before I get sick. The constant worries over getting sick. In Guibert's novel,

always a worry of bodily collapse and then the book is unfinished. "I'm actually writing all of this on the evening of January
3 because I'm afraid I'll collapse during the night . . . pressing on
fiercely towards my goal and towards its incompletion . . ." The
concept of a deadline seems too on the nose. I put that Guibert quote next to this one from Bakhtin's *Rabelais and His World*:
"It is ambivalent. It is pregnant death, a death that gives birth.
There is nothing completed, nothing calm and stable in the
bodies of these old hags. They combine a senile, decaying and
deformed flesh with the flesh of new life, conceived but as yet
unformed. Life is shown in its two-fold contradictory process;
it is the epitome of incompleteness. And such is the grotesque
concept of the body."

The countless articles wondering if pregnant women are high-
risk. I read that my immune system is compromised because
there's someone else's DNA inside of me. I worry food has lost all
taste—is it my sinuses, this pregnancy, or a symptom of the virus?
Dysgeusia, it's called. I worry I will die at the temporary field
hospital erected at the Javits Center, which was to host the corporate yearly publishing expo that I would have been expected
to sign books at, or worse, die at the field hospital run by bigots
in Central Park. I worry also I will give birth at the Javits Center. Partners have been banned from labor and delivery rooms.
One gives birth alone, in a mask. We drive through the tunnel
from Brooklyn to the empty West Side Highway to the Fetal
Maternal Evaluation Ward for a full anatomy ultrasound. My
temperature is taken from six feet away by a nurse outfitted like
an astronaut. It is not a form of protective chic, like Guibert's
descriptions of the nurses at the Institut Alfred-Fournier like out
of Yves St. Laurent, as Andrew Durbin points out. "With semisheer stockings and flats, straight skirts, and tasteful necklaces

worn over their white smocks, the nurses look very chic, more like piano teachers or bank officers. They slip on their latex gloves as though they were velvet gloves for a gala evening at the opera." Barricades of chairs in front of the receptionist's desk. Most of the chairs are taken away from the lobby. Four tired pregnant women in masks and with bottles of water stare at each other. I have tucked a notebook in the pocket of my coat, but I don't feel I can write in it. I feel total blankness. My medical gloves itch—I sense even then it's overkill wearing them. I observe that the only medical personnel not now given a medical-grade mask—but mint-green to match–is the woman who wheels out the blood-pressure machine. She's also the only one who's nice to me, and who actually touches me, because she has to. I had to keep on asking to have my blood pressure taken, and she comes with her machine, wrapping the band around my arm, filling it up with the pump. The ultrasound tech won't talk to me or call the baby a munchkin like my previous ones did. I still am desperate to chat with the tech, even if she's mostly unresponsive, most likely because she's severely stressed. Is she here? Here? Are those the toes? Before I get to the hospital I get an email from the midwives to all of their patients—the changes that will happen over these months as I move into the third trimester—for now, we will have to labor in a mask, the partner can now be there but will have to leave two hours after delivery, we are regarded as suspicious the whole time as test results won't be back, and if we're positive the baby gets taken away to the ICU . . .

In one of the most haunting passages at the opening of the novel, Guibert details a Sisphyean transit across Paris to the Hôpital Claude-Bernard amidst the deserted streets of Paris paralyzed by a taxi strike, to get his blood drawn, for the pre-AZT check, the results of which begin the time clock for his narration of his illness in the opening movement of the novel. He has to crowd himself into a suffocating Métro car, only coffee in his stomach, not able to eat because of the blood work. The hospital felt, he wrote, like "a phantom hospital at the end of the earth," surrounded by fog, like his visit to Dachau (more holocaustal imagery). The weaving labyrinth of the streets of Paris and the gray and brutal landscape of an abandoned hospital. There's a horror feel to the scene. The empty maze of the hospital from which he wishes to escape. So much like the hysteria of the waiting room at La Salpêtrière in Rainer Maria Rilke's *Notebooks of Malte Laurids Brigge*, the extreme fear of the death that waits in all of us. "The nurse who was supposed to draw my blood gave me a look filled with sweetness that meant, 'You're going to die before me.'" He has vial after vial drained from him. How long and sweeping his sentences and pages, like the halls and corridors of the hospital.

PANIC

We've become paranoid of contact with other people. All of the rumors as to how it's transmitted. Wash your hands after you touch money, John's mother texts him from Michigan. We wonder where she gets her misinformation from, maybe Facebook, somewhere even more suspect than Fox News. Feels bound up in elaborate anti-Semitic cabals regarding financiers. That devastating scene in *Close to the Knives*, when the diner owner makes Peter Hujar, who is dying from AIDS, put his money in a paper bag. It's become embedded in us, this fear of others, of being infected, of any intimacy with the outside. We fervently disinfect doorknobs. Leave our mail unopened. Tell the delivery person nervously to leave it on the stoop. John tells Leo not to sit on our bench outside or on park benches. We stop going to the park—the crowds make us nervous. On our daily circum-ambulation with the dog, we urge Leo not to touch anything, spraying sanitizer on our hands when we brush up against any foreign surfaces, trying to measure out how to stay six feet away. We begin washing our hands all the time, until they crack out of dryness, talking to our daughter about germs, we watch videos together on how best to wash hands. One day, a knock on the door. Our dog goes crazy, as usual. Alarmed, we ask, who is it? One of the girls upstairs, I try to trace out whether she's standing six feet away. Monika—who I like, young, thirty, a writer—has a cough and a 102 fever. She can't get a test, of course. They're sending over Tamiflu. Why didn't she email? John is annoyed. I email her, tell her to take Vitamin D, ask if she wants us to leave out Gatorade and cold medicine. I order something called Fire Cider online—a tonic of apple cider vinegar, horseradish, onion, ginger, turmeric, habanero pepper. We take shots of it to bolster our immunity. After he dies, Muzil's partner fervently disinfects the home, the passage also describes his revulsion at finding the closet of S&M paraphernalia, making it more clear that AIDS was a moral revulsion, dealing with what Julia Kristeva, also read-ing Mary Douglas on the impure in *Powers of Horror*, situates as the abject, the repulsion towards body fluids. Muzil had managed to spare his partner from contracting the virus, Guibert writes, even though they weren't aware how contagious his body was, the poison of his saliva, sperm, tears, and sweat, showing the fictions spread in the novel, written at the height of AIDS panic, mak-ing this a live document that's a time capsule, showing the sub-jectivity of paranoia and panic, even for those inflicted, of these bodily fluids listed only semen actually transmits HIV, as well as breast milk, vaginal fluid, and anal mucus, and of course blood, the blood that abounds in Guibert's novel. I am reminded, rather inappropriately, of the skit my daughter started to perform at this time, from Charlie Brown, that scene where Snoopy kisses Lucy, she tears around screaming Argghh!!! Get some Disinfectant! Get some Iodine!

VITALS

The midwife wants to do a Zoom "visit" as opposed to seeing me in person. I do it from my bed. I don't wash my face or change out of my stretched-out nightromper, which has holes in the crotch. She is in a full gown, head covering, scrubs, mask. She appears to be calling from the hospital where she is delivering a baby. She seems to be sitting in a hallway. I ask her if she feels comfortable at the hospital now. She says she does. She says it's overblown, the nightmare in the news—of stretchers of the dead outside New York hospitals, of nurses and doctors not having PPE, instead wearing trash bags. She can't take any of my vitals, I haven't gotten my blood pressure cuff yet. I want to ask if she thinks by my due date I will still have to give birth wearing a mask but I don't. It seems asinine to worry about that when she's risking her life.

It's cool and gray outside. It was just Easter weekend. There's so much birdsong lately, as if the birds are suddenly free to come out, the city quiet except for the ambulance sirens at all hours. There are green buds on trees during our brief walk around the block before dusk. My throat itches, is it from sinuses, from allergies? I can't breathe through the mask because my nose is too stuffed up. The bloody tissues every morning. The small discomforts don't register anymore amidst the trauma and suffering of so many. Countless articles online—there's no possible way out of it. The dreadful news. The global death toll about 100,000 (the number of deaths from AIDS in NYC). Every day now at the height of this 600–800 die in the city, most likely undercounted, probably a thousand a day, so many more dying at home. 5,000 in ICUs. 170,000 confirmed cases in New York. But it's impossible to get tested. So we must live with the suspension and dread of waiting, of not knowing. The sight and sound of the ambulance on our street, it never leaves. The extreme grief and anonymity of these deaths. Dying on a ventilator like being drowned alive. Forty percent of the dead are in nursing homes. No mourners allowed at their bedside. No funerals. It makes Foucault's desire for death's anonymity, his fantasy of disappearing behind a painting in a nursing home, tonally off. *Hardly even a number on a slip of paper.* Muzil's wracking cough. That is the fear. The cough. The dry, hard cough. Shortness of breath. And the constant low-grade fever that can suddenly spike. Haunting threads of paranoid hallucinations, severe cardiac and respiratory symptoms. The cognitive symptoms like the unending brain fog. The brutality of it. The way it wrecks your immune system. In the newspaper, photographs of ditches being dug at Hart's Island, the historic potter's field, unmarked graves stacked like blocks. The white against black. The long empty rows of graves—the future. Thousands of those who died of AIDS were buried there, dug by Riker's Island inmates, who are now also dying of this virus, trapped in obscenely unsanitary conditions as the virus spreads. One man who attended a dinner, a birthday party, and a funeral in Chicago is the source of transmission of 15 infected people, three deaths. The virus "preys on the human propensity to connect."

GARGOYLES

My author copies for the novel arrive from my publisher. I don't open the box for weeks, shove it under the table. Still the contagion-feeling of mail. Strange to have it not be in bookstores, for no one to be able to get the physical copy for a while. I love the opening of Bernhard's *Wittgenstein's Nephew*, the nuns place a copy of his recently published *Gargoyles* on his hospital bed. The uneasy and absurd feeling of this, amidst everything. I am not writing lately, paralyzed by what that even means anymore. What does language mean during a crisis? But especially, why write first-person books? The Guibert still feels to me like an essential document, from within (a community, a body). The bodily, adamant, even cruel or hysterical first-person writing of illness fiercely opposes the medical gaze, opposes the absolute anonymity of death. A refusal to disappear. To react against the small moments of coercion, of shaming in the medical process. A document of fear and dread and still beauty—staring at horror, what is its face?

ATTEMPT

As I sit here one morning at the desk in the front room attempting to figure out why I'm so obsessed with Hervé Guibert, with his book, with this study, with writing and its relationship to death, Leo brings out a sheet of computer paper and her markers, and begins making what she calls notes next to me, little bird-like wing scrawls. "Keep on writing, Mommy," she says to me when I stop and look at her, amused. I'm waiting for my coffee, I say to her. She goes into the other room, to her toy kitchen, to make me pretend coffee to drink, which she brings in her small blue wooden mug. Makes herself a plate of tiny wooden toast, to mirror mine. "I'm going to do some work while I'm eating."

I close the laptop, ask her what she's writing. She's writing about safety, she says. Never run into the street. Don't go off with strangers. Don't go into deep water. Do you remember before the virus? This is how she now situates time. We have conversations about it daily. There is a virus going around . . . is the virus still going around? A half-hour passes. I only had an hour this morning. I make a note with red pen in the margins of my typed notes. When I do this, Leo selects a purple marker and carefully makes a scrawl as well. I look at the dolls she's placed, slumped over, on the chairs next to me. All of the tableaux of her dolls left around the apartment that remind me of one of Guibert's favorite photographic subjects, the wax dolls in museums that he also collected.

That one photograph of him, his curly mop, taking a photograph in an askew mirror, a marionette suspended above him like it's being hanged. One of my favorite Guibert photographs, from a brief visit to New York in 1981, a girl in a patterned dress frozen in mid-pose/dancing amidst the glass cases of Degas bronzes. His photograph of the operatic struggle between two wax dolls. Even when he photographs Isabelle Adjani, there's a waxen quality to her. I help Leo find her doll's rattle, her doll's headband, I can locate all of these in her room in my brain, what other memories or thoughts have been pushed out so as to track and recreate the ever-shifting chaos of her room so exactly, she leaves with her father and the dog for a walk, I have twenty minutes now. I have a Braxton-Hicks contraction. I waddle to pee. I repeat this. I spend most of my time on the toilet. An hour and a half later. I have coaxed Leo through her half-hour Zoom dance class, then eaten a plate of scrambled eggs and more toast. Scarves, Simon Says, banging on drums, first position. I am exhausted. I move from the kitchen table to the couch, now to the desk, summoning a little more energy, attempting.

NOVEL

Later in May the stream of interviews, sometimes in the form of "events" I conduct over Zoom to promote the book, massive and heavily breathing on the couch, or in the armchair, my face gleaming with sweat. The domestic clutter or carefully arranged spaces that we peer into, everyone's rooms. I wonder what Guibert would have thought about these camera glimpses we get at others' spaces, either disorganized or carefully curated. Why is your book a novel? I am often asked. I keep on repeating the same script, the novel is a capacious form, it can take on diaries, essays, letters, poetry . . . I also talk about Hervé Guibert the entire time. This is what he said in an interview when asked this:

> When I got the proofs I had doubts. Was it really a novel? Everything is scrupulously accurate and I started from real characters, real ones, I needed real ones to be able to write. But as I wrote and though I did not rework anything (I had not the heart even to go over the proofs), I covered my tracks . . . That said, the book is also a novel. Muzil, Marine and the others are characters, after all, they are not quite as they are in real life. Even the person who is Hervé Guibert in the book is a character.

PROTEST

All throughout June I keep on going back to the question of activism and writing. Which is also a question of egotism versus the collective—the I versus the we. Across the country daily protests—for weeks, months—spurred by the murder of George Floyd, a Black man brutally killed by the police, following so many other Black people who have been brutalized and killed by police, including Breonna Taylor killed in her bed. The police beat peaceful protesters—tear-gas and pepper-spray them, blind several protesters and journalists, drive into crowds. The ambulance sirens now replaced by constant helicopters overhead. We take Leo to protests for families with children, marching slowly down Ocean Avenue in our masks. Along with our neighbors we bang on pots and pans and Leo's musical instruments to protest the curfew imposed to further criminalize the protests. There is such a hopefulness now in the air, but it is a rending feeling—of the possibility of revolution and change, there is talk now of abolishing the police, also of connection and catharsis. I am glad to be in Brooklyn, to not have left. To be witness to this collective action, which a plague cannot suppress.

AGAINST GUIBERT

I wonder often why I chose Hervé Guibert as the subject for a study and not David Wojnarowicz, a writer and artist and activist who in many ways I admire more, even love more, for his anger and grace. In many ways David Wojnarowicz was a saint, the way elegy and political rage comingle in his life and work. Guibert was not a saint, even though, I think, he's been made into a saint, by those who misunderstand the thrust and negative energy of his work. Or then again, maybe thinking who is or not a saint is some fucked-up latent and reactive Catholicism, a moralizing narrative onto literature that is so much part of the capitalist project of publishing, the sanctimonious refrain. Perhaps it's because I am still struggling to understand Guibert, and to understand in a way the urgency of first-person narrative at all when writing about the body and experience when the world is falling apart, as it was then and still is now. Didier Lestrade, one of the founders of ACT-UP Paris, wrote an essay, translated as "Against Guibert," critiquing his writing as being an "individual adventure," saying his suffering did not make him a humanist. And it's true, Guibert was not an activist, and probably can't be best described as a humanist. There is a lot of cringey casual racism in the novel (the references to the "Chinese flu," how he glibly quotes Muzil writing about the disease being from Africa). He doesn't say much about the care of others, or their inability to get care, versus his own status as a celebrity, which he attempts to exploit to get special treatment, to be cured with the experimental vaccine. There is an extreme privilege to the friend group he is writing about, even though the friends have been devastated by the disease, a dismissal of abuse as Sadean excesses (especially the pedophilic references in his journals, namely about his friend Robin who goes regularly for sex tourism to Thailand, which disturb me to the point that I skip over them, a character mentioned in dinner scenes later in the novel). He is writing about community, portraits of others, friendships, at times with vitriol and other times tenderness, sometimes these two feelings comingled, although his writing is antisocial, parasitic, reactive, often anti-humanist. But Guibert also offers himself up as an instrument, rewriting the loss of identity under the medical gaze, under the homophobic gaze through these early AIDS treatments. He's writing of the urgency of the body and his own subjectivity. He was one of the first to write so nakedly about having AIDS, and his fame afterwards, the way his image was disseminated, is because he became something of an icon for those who were also suffering silently and privately. He wrote honestly of the daily suffering of illness, the desire and drive towards both life as well as suicide, as opposed to the cool remove with which Sontag wished to write about cancer, removing herself from her experience. Something of the reactionariness and humidity of his work speaks against the dehumanizing discourse of AIDS, its language of contamination, the way that AIDS patients, including Guibert, were treated. There is a refusal to be shamed, to be private or modest (to quote the title of his film), or when the shame does creep in, a refusal to be stopped from writing through this shame.

MAZE

In his documentation of the constant monitoring of blood work and T4 levels, of getting lost going to various remote isolated infectious wards for this or that test, he is also critiquing the tedium of being a patient, the bureaucratic hoops he must jump through in order to qualify for both public and secret protocols, a series of mazes like out of Kafka. In this first of his AIDS novels, the process of qualifying for AZT in France is unbearably bureaucratic. He must wait for his blood work to see if he has been approved by the committee (with a note that the government was worried that patients would try to sell their drugs to the Africans, where the narrator notes, in a flash of political awareness, the governments just let their AIDS patients die). By the second novel, he has to endure waiting to qualify for the DDI protocol, and so must resort to theft and the black market in which to secure it. The attempts to secure the retrovirals to extend his life are a drive throughout each book. AZT, the clinical name Zidovudine, was an experimental chemotherapy drug derived from the semen of herring and salmon, developed twenty-five years earlier and shelved because it was both so toxic and so expensive to produce, and ultimately not therapeutic for cancer patients. But it became the first hope for AIDS patients, approved by the FDA on March 20, 1987, following the results of a study that would later be declared invalid. The pharmaceutical company, Burroughs Wellcome, which made the drug made $230 million in profit in the second year after it was marketed to HIV and AIDS patients. It was said to cost $10,000 for a one-year supply in the States. It is now questioned whether AZT (or any of the antiviral monotherapies) did anything to prolong the life of patients, and in the end it may have compounded their illnesses. Combination therapy, or the AIDS cocktail, was not made available until 1995, and it remains prohibitively expensive in the States, especially without insurance, as pharmaceutical companies are still obscenely profiting off those living with HIV or seeking to incubate themselves from HIV (including Gilead, which makes the HIV preventative drug, Truvada, or PrEP, which costs thousands a month without insurance, which has now begun marketing the antiviral HIV drug Remdesivir to COVID-19 patients, planning to charge $3,000 for a full course of treatment, the first drug that was FDA-approved, even though its efficacy is debated). It is no coincidence that the real villain of *To the Friend*, Bill, the fifty-year-old pharmaceutical executive, is based out of Miami, and is hoping to make tremendous profits off of an experimental AIDS vaccine pioneered by Mockney, a character based off of Jonas Salk, the inventor of the polio vaccine, who at the time was promising a vaccine using the deactivated virus, and just needed volunteers, even offering to inject himself, as well as seeking out celibate priests and nuns as potential subjects. Bill is the one who holds the promised salvation at the opening, the titular friend who did not save his life, namely that he'll let the Guibert narrator, Jules, and Berthe into the double-blind trial, as long as he keeps his T count above 300, but manipulate it so that they received the promised vaccine, a grift that he keeps up throughout the novel, before ultimately ghosting him. This is a depressing repetition in AIDS narratives at this time, these fraudulent promises of miracle cures. For enough money, of course. I think of a dying Peter Hujar insisting that David Wojnarowicz take him to a quack doctor holding shop in a Long Island trailer where he would inject AIDS patients with typhoid, theorizing that this would bolster their immune system, something Wojnarowicz documents scathingly in the most devastating essay in *Close to the Knives*, where the critique extends from the cruelty of the American health care system to capitalism itself. With Guibert's novel, his personal struggle and the struggles of those in his circle remain the focus—it reads as a work about one man attempting to use whatever resources he can to survive, even attempting, in the follow-up novel, to use his newfound celebrity to secure more drugs. And there is within the incendiary critique that within this schema, the gay person with AIDS—even a famous one, even a *name*—was made to seem and feel expendable.

FUCK YOU, BILL!

By the last movement all of the narrator's energy and hatred is directed towards Bill, as the sections become shorter and more staccato, hypoxic with rage, taking on a speed and momentum, as if he must finish the book in order to out Bill as the con man, capitalist pig, and, it's more than inferred, closeted pederast that he is. Bill, with his red Ferrari and series of disposable boys, who promises that he will hook up his friend with the vaccine is paranoid in clandestine meetings, including a bizarro scene of them going to see *Empire of the Sun* together, starring a baby-faced Christian Bale, giving the last movement the feel of a noir. This conspiracy is unraveled in more dinners within their shared friend group. "Just as AIDS will have been my paradigm in my project of self-revelation and the expression of the inexpressible, AIDS will prove to be the perfect model for the secret of Bill's entire life. AIDS has allowed him to take the role of master of ceremonies in our little group of friends, which he manipulates as though it were a kind of scientific experiment." Bill who made him dance in front of him with a hard-on for eighteen months, exposing the results of his T4 count, there was nothing more naked or exposing than that. Jules is so furious at this treachery he suggests that his lover put a drop of his blood in a wineglass during dinner (they are still having dinners together). He last sees Bill the day after going to the hospital to get his blood work, on December 23. "But he was tired, and so was I, and it was as though neither of us believed anymore in the possibility of this vaccine and its power to bring my disease under control, as though, in the end, languidly, we no longer gave a damn, just didn't give a fucking damn." The last fragment on the last page, section 100, is like that drop of blood in the wineglass, before disintegration, one last "fuck you, Bill!" which was for a time the working title of the novel.

> My book is closing in on me. I'm in deep shit. Just how deep do you want me to sink? Fuck you, Bill! My muscles have melted away. At last my arms and legs are once again as slender as they were when I was a child.

KINETIC SAND

Again I write about Guibert while waiting—in suspension. I have two months before the baby comes. There are fireworks in June for hours at night, sometimes sustained and other times sporadic—helicopters still circling—increasing the paranoia on top of the isolation. No one sleeps. Farfetched theories circulate that the fireworks at all hours are government psyops in reaction to the ongoing protests. Theories both born and believed by collective sleeplessness. I try to nap during the day. How hot and uncomfortable I am. I walk around in a pair of striped overalls that make me look like the rainbow parachute at a Gymboree. My body is ballooning. At home I only wear underwear. How my belly now hardens, peaks. The turning and twisting being inside. Constant diarrhea. Back pain. One night I worry my contractions are real, not the false ones that warm up the uterus. I call the midwife, who tells me to have a drink and take some magnesium. I have a finger of whisky in the bathtub. It is the most relaxed I've felt this entire pregnancy. How sore and slow I am now. I need to lie down most of the time, on my side. With the family I take brief walks outside in the heat. I feel ancient. I have stopped eating large meals, I can only eat snacks. Constant acid reflux as the baby is sitting on my diaphragm. Yogurt. An egg. Fruit.

There is a sense of crossing over. There is a month left now. The other day I watched Leo play with hot pink kinetic sand for an hour. Watching her stretch it in her hands, ball it, pound it. I order up neon tempera paints for her, watch her swirl paint around on a large sheet of paper. Such a doubling to this confinement. The loop of time. The extreme heat keeps me inside as well. I collapse on the couch. Stomach cleaving in two. Weeks left. During Leo's nap I rally myself, stretch, bounce on my feet. The mere accumulation of pages some sort of feat. That I transcended time. That I wrote something of the facts of the body. I wait to go into labor. I read statistics of birth being described as a mortality event in one of the endless articles about the virus. The unit of measure, a micromort, registers a one in a million chance of dying. Skydiving is seven micromorts per jump. Going under anesthesia is five micromorts. Living in New York City during the virus carries with it 50 micromorts of risk daily. Giving birth in the United States, by contrast, is 210 micromorts—the article doesn't parse how this risk of mortality intersects with race and class, which severely exacerbate this vulnerability. Beginning next week, I will go for regular stress tests and ultrasounds at the hospital. I have three more weeks to go, or less. I gave an interview last week for a podcast. I spoke about how when I am approaching labor, as I am now, I think of death the entire time. Partially because birth feels so close to death. Not only because of the risks of maternal mortality. My body is slowing down, heavy, I can only eat small meals, just like my mother when she was dying. I am visited more by ghosts, near the end. Still, at the end of all of this, I don't know why, when I speak about writing, I am speaking about death. Since childbirth especially, when I realized I could die, realized my mortality and vulnerability. That a body could be stopped at any time. I still haven't answered one of my questions hovering over all of this. How does writing change, once one knows that one is going to die? In my notebook I have written down this quote from Kathy Acker: "I'm no superstar shit and never will be. If anything, I'm what happens after death, which is writing."

SURGE

Still there is something beautiful to this dailiness. Every day is the same. Every day is Leo, all day. An hour or two of thinking about Guibert stretched out. A quote I write down from Etel Adnan's *Surge*: "Thinking takes time, and probably resembles time, as we can't figure out what each is, and how they interact, and resemble themselves." A nap at midday. Difficulty showering, getting out of the bathtub. I gulp down liquids, alternating Gatorade and water. I watch Guibert's home video, shot at the end of his life, screened on French television in January 1992. He shot it between June 1990 and March 1991. *La Pudeur ou L'impudeur. Modesty, or Immodesty*. Immodesty also translated to Shamelessness. My copy doesn't have subtitles. I can't decipher most of his voiceover, delivered in the same monotone voice as his talk show appearance, so the one-hour film for me is mostly mute, which makes it even more present, bodily. It's difficult to parse how time passes. We are mostly inside interiors, his Paris apartment, medical offices, his villa in Elba. The same objects become totems. Are we on a loop of the same repetition of days, the life of a dying person, or does he loop in the scenes from the same time period? There is the red armchair in his Parisian apartment next to his bookshelf we keep returning to, he sits talking on the phone, notebooks and mail on the floor, his bony long foot. Is it later in the day he's on the same chair, hand over face, napping? The repetition of clinician scenes, just like they are on repeat in the novel—slowly rolling up his baggy blazer to get blood taken, on his back on a hospital bed speaking to a white coat. The endless waiting and silence. Close-up of his skeletal frame, seemingly skinnier over time. Scenes of exercising in his apartment. On a stationary bike. Boxing at the camera. Squats. Slow, exaggerated movement. A masseuse works on his naked frame, delicate and slim as a child's. He speaks of his fatigue. Shot of his body, on the bed. Throughout, shots of him on the toilet, face in his hands, suffering from diarrhea. On his desk piles of files, negatives, manuscripts, notebooks. A reoccurring scene of pouring powder into a glass in his bathroom. The mise en scène of medical supplies.

The film captures the slowness of the day, versus the speed, the energy of the page of *To the Friend*. A meditation on age and dying. Interspersed throughout are his interviews with his two ninety-something aunts, Suzanne and Louise, as they speak of sickness and dying while laying in bed. Contrasted with a shot of two blond children on a boat, the various positions of their stuffed animals on their pillows (I assume they are the children of Thierry and Christine, who Guibert married after Thierry's death so she and the children could receive his royalties). Another counterpoint—his skinny limbs showering, trying to wash himself from behind. It's hard to watch his emaciated frame. When I last saw Moyra Davey in December, we spoke about the film. He was so courageous to make it, she said to me. I think about

that, about Guibert's courage. A refusal to disappear while showing the deterioration of his body, his energy. Modesty *or* immodesty. He chooses immodesty. The delicacy and horror of his naked
body, his ribs. The truth of dying. He seems so completely isolated, except for medical personnel and the other people he pays
to touch him. The ongoingness of his days, how small they are,
repetitive and dragging as a unit of time. An empty fridge. The
swirling of the laundry machine. He slowly eats a jar of yogurt.
Attempts to sit upright at his desk, tapping at his typewriter,
surrounded by manuscripts and notebooks. A rather horrifying
scene of being prepared for surgery, he is covered in sheets, the
doctors in masks and full protective equipment, he is faceless,
unconscious, a reference perhaps to Rembrandt's *Anatomy Lesson*.
Still the murmur of the doctors as they perform surgery on his
unconscious body and we pan to Guibert sitting in a chair, seemingly watching himself, like a ghost. He walks around his beautiful Parisian apartment, listening to music. The stuffed monkey on
a bureau. His statues and books. Watching out the window onto
the street, people running by (a marathon?).

Halfway through the film he gets on a plane to Elba. The landscape of the countryside. Stone church. His villa. Whitewashed
walls. Rustic furniture. Chandeliers we'll later see lit at night.
Candles. The stern faces of his paintings. Another desk. So many
spots of solitude. Painterly shots, like still lifes. Outward gaze.
A close-up of a frog. A bird. Hills. Flipping through his diary.
A lizard on a half-eaten apple. A basket of fruit. Guibert eats
an egg out of a cup slowly. Later he's eating a piece of fruit. The
reoccurrence of a balloon twisting in the wind. A butterfly hovering inside (*grand papillon*). Rustling of trees. Sheets in the wind.
Still on toilet, head in his hands. An extended scene in which he
shows us one of the vials of digitalis he's purchased to commit

suicide. The tableau of his desk. A marionette. A large green glass bottle of water. He puts the digitalis in his drink with a dropper. He looks at the glass. He drinks from it. Intercut by the slow twisting of a mosquito net. Twisting of his suspended elephant statue. The rustling of newspapers in the wind. Here in Italy he sits and naps in the blue armchair. He wakes up. He reads. He is still alive. The rocky beach. Naked going into the water. Just when I am wondering—is it possible he's entirely alone? he's carried on the back of a companion. Back in Paris. Opening mail on a red chair. A medical appointment. They make small talk, she listens to his breathing. A shot of an empty wheelchair. At the end, the sound of the alarm clock, swinging legs over to get out of bed. At the desk working. Coughing, typing. It seems unbearable, this existence. Unbearable and ordinary and private and isolating. He will make it through almost the entire year before ending his life. Always writing, or trying to write. As a way to prevent death? As a way to look it in the eye? I wonder if death is the ultimate betrayal, not writing. Writing a way to mark an "I" before it is extinguished.

I keep having this fantasy that turns out to come true, the pandemic is over, the virus is gone, we are all free to travel. I am free, unencumbered. I finally can travel alone. I book a ticket for Rome and make my way to Elba—several train rides and a boat ride. I book a room in a villa close to where Guibert lived. I make a pilgrimage to his grave. I sit on the rocky beach. I eat fruit. I write in my notebook. I write the Guibert study now, finally, slowly. I have all the time in the world. Hours every day. Someone comes and cooks and cleans for me. It is warm here. The air is beautiful. I don't know why you don't believe me, but this really did happen. It did. I wrote you a postcard—did it not arrive?

ACKNOWLEDGMENTS

I want to acknowledge the community of readers and writers who first read my writing and encouraged me—many of whom I am lucky to be in conversation with still, and others who, even though there's been an absence of many years, I think about often with love and admiration. In addition to the writer I write towards in the first section of these pages, I want to thank Rebecca Loudon, Angela Simione, Gina Abelkop, Kate Durbin, Suzanne Scanlon, Amina Cain, and others, my first cherished writing community. As always, to Sofia Samatar, who was a crucial reader, early interlocuter, and supporter of this book. Many of the quotes and ideas littered throughout this book were given to me by you, the far smarter reader. To Danielle Dutton for her advice and support, and for continually encouraging me that this book was worth writing. Gratitude and admiration to Amy Hollywood, for your mind and for being such an enthusiastic reader of this book and previous work. To Moyra Davey, for your conversation about Hervé Guibert, for your belief in me and this project, and for the incredible influence of your work. Sorry for stealing your titling! Also thank you for sending me your copy of Sophie Calle's *Exquisite Pain* in the mail during a pandemic! To other writers I deeply admire whose thinking on Guibert has inspired me—including Brian Blanchfield, Andrew Durbin, Janique Vigier, Renee Gladman, and Clutch Fleischmann. Including my beyond brilliant nonfiction graduate students at Columbia University, especially my "On Time" seminar, who thought through this Guibert novel with me in the fall of 2020. Especially Will Harrison, for your own thinking and writing on Guibert, Hannah Gold, for your conversation and help with Leo over the years, and to Anamarie Pasdar, for making me laugh and helping me stay sane parenting a newborn and a preschooler during a pandemic, and for taking Leo into your home when I gave birth. To Philomene Cohen, for all of your assistance on this book—including your wonderful translations, fact-checking, research, art insights, and your invaluable work on the endnotes. To The Robert B. Silvers Foundation for a grant of $2,500, which allowed me to continue work on this book in September and October of 2020. To Hedi El Kholti, for publishing my first-person in the past and for encouraging me to write this study. To Mel Flashman, for your enthusiasm towards this project. To Harriet Moore, for your energy and poetic insight. To Cal Morgan, for your continued belief in my work. To everyone at Columbia University Press, but especially Jenny Davidson, who championed this book's weird forms from the beginning, and Philip Leventhal, for his fortitude and patience, Marielle T. Poss and Ben Kolstad for overseeing the production and copyediting, Julia Kushnirsky for designing the book's jacket, and to Caitlin Hurst, publicist extraordinaire. To Matthew Lange, the Sarah Charlesworth Estate, and Paula Cooper Gallery, for the use of Sarah Charlesworth's haunting *Skull* for the cover. To my partner, the writer and artist John Vincler, for his continued support of my work, for his careful edits and conversation, and for watching our daughters Leo and Rainer so that I could attempt this study in the spare pockets of time that neither of us have had. I'd also like to express profound gratitude for the midwives who delivered Rainer and took care of me during pregnancy and postpartum, while working out of a New York hospital during a plague—Jenna Sood, Christina McPherson, and Elaine Keller-Duemig—for their extreme sacrifice in caring for me and others with patience, love, and humor, in these sometimes scary and speculative conditions, and for making sure I survived.

This book is dedicated to Bhanu Kapil, whose writing and thinking, in her books, letters, and blog, have catalyzed my own work, and for her friendship over the past decade, which continues to be a lifeline.

NOTES

ABBREVIATIONS OF PRINCIPAL EDITIONS USED

Guibert, Hervé. *Compassion Protocol*. Translated by James Kirkup. London: Quartet Books, October 1993. Referred to as *Compassion*.

———. *The Mausoleum of Lovers*. Translated by Nathanaël. Brooklyn: Nightboat Books, 2014. Referred to as *Mausoleum*.

———. *To the Friend Who Did Not Save My Life*. Translated by Linda Coverdale. London: Serpent's Tail, 1993. Reprint, New York: Semiotext(e): 2020. Referred to as *To the Friend*. (Page numbers correspond to the Semiotext(e) edition.)

Apostrophes. "Hervé Guibert 'A l'ami qui ne m'a pas sauvé la vie.'" trans. Philo Cohen. *INA Archives* video. 14:51, March 16, 1991. Referred to as *Apostrophes*.

"Disappearance" Part I

p.3 "In the years of friendship . . .": Bruce Boone, *Century of Clouds* (Brooklyn: Nightboat Books, 2009), 3.

p.6 "Do you believe you are the first man to find yourself . . .": Charles Baudelaire, *Lettres: 1841–1866*, trans. Philo Cohen (Paris: Société du Mercure de France, 1907), 364.

p.9 W.G. Sebald, *Austerlitz*, trans. Anthea Bell (New York: Penguin Random House, 2001), 3.

p.10   "no one of which is original: the text is a tissue of citations":
Roland Barthes, "The Death of The Author," trans. Stephen Heath,
in *Image, Music, Text* (New York: Hill and Wang, 1978), 160.

p.10   Charles Baudelaire, "Brussels Spleen," trans. Richard Sieburth,
Conjunctions (Spring 2014).

p.11   "I consider it useless and tedious . . .": Baudelaire, "Salon of
1859," trans. Jonathan Mayne, in *Charles Baudelaire, The Mirror of Art*
(London: Phaidon Press Limited, 1956), 233.

p.11   "kind of vertigo, something of a 'detective anguish'": Barthes,
Camera Lucida, trans. Richard Howard (New York: Hill and Wang,
1981), 85.

p.12   "The public would see . . .": *To the Friend*, 33.

p.12   "designer death resort": *ibid*, 30.

p.12   "Everything there should be . . .": *ibid*, 30.

p.13   "Rather, it is primarily concerned . . .": Michel Foucault, "What
Is an Author?", trans. Josue V. Harari, in *Foucault Reader*, ed. Paul
Rabinow (New York: Random House, 1984), 301.

p.13   "Don't pull the Max Brod-Kafka trick . . .": John Forrester,
"Foucault's Face: The Personal Is the Theoretical," *Foucault Now:
Current Perspectives in Foucault Studies*, ed. James D. Faubion (Cam-
bridge: Polity Press, 2014), 113.

p.14   "The painting didn't reveal . . .": *To the Friend*, 74.

p.15   "And all of this great hollow space . . .": Foucault, *Manet and the
Object of Painting*, trans. Matthew Barr (London: Tate, 2009), 63.

p.16   Elizabeth H. Jones, *Spaces of Belonging: "Home, Culture and
Identity in 20th-Century French Autobiography"* (Amsterdam, Neth-
erlands:: Rodopi, 2007), 146.

p.17   "a strange feeling came upon me": W.G. Sebald, *Rings of Saturn*,
trans. Michael Hulse (New York: New Directions, 2016), 183.

p.18   "For days and weeks on end . . .": *ibid*, 181.

p.20   "The day was overcast . . ." *To the Friend*, 117.

p.20   "the outlines and rough drafts . . ." *ibid*, 117.

p.21   Guibert, "Ghost Image", in *Ghost Image*, trans. Robert Bononno
(Chicago: University of Chicago Press, 2014).

p.21 "by drawing a circle . . ." *ibid*, 118.

p.31 Renee Gladman, *Calamities* (Seattle, WA: Wave, 2016).

p.22 "I haven't done a stitch of work . . ." *To the Friend*, 70.

p.23 "Each book up to now . . .": André Gide, *Journals*. Vol. 1: 1889–1913, trans. Justin O'Brien (Urbana: University of Illinois Press, 2000), 243.

p.25 Giorgio Agamben, "Identity Without A Person," in *Nudities*, trans. David Kishik and Stefan Pedatella, (Stanford, CA: Stanford University Press, 2011), 13.

p.28 "I will propose a game . . .": Foucault, "The Masked Philosopher," trans. John Johnston, in *Foucault Live*, ed. Sylvère Lotringer (New York: Semiotext(e), 1989), 193.

p.28 "Muzil had become obsessed . . .": *To the Friend*, 31.

p.28 "What flash of insight . . .": *ibid*, 31.

p.29 Tehching Hsieh, *Out Now*, ed. Adrian Heathfield (Cambridge: The MIT Press, 2015).

p.29 Lisa Chen, Eugene Lim, and Anelise Chen, "An Interview with Tehching Hsieh," *The Believer*, April 1, 2019.

p.31 Renee Gladman also writes about the tonal qualities of *To the Friend Who Did Not Save My Life* in *To After That (Toaf)* (Berkeley, CA. Atelos, 2008).

p.32 Claudia Rankine, *Don't Let Me Be Lonely* (Minneapolis, MN: Graywolf Press, September 2004), 130.

p.33 "What strikes me is the fact that in our society   ": Foucault, "On the Genealogy of Ethics: An Overview of Work in Progress," in *Foucault Reader*, ed. Paul Rabinow, (New York: Pantheon, 1984), 350.

p.33 Foucault, "Self Writing", in *Ethics, Subjectivity and Truth*, ed. Paul Rabinow (New York: New Press, May 1998).

p.39 "a relationship that is still formless . . .": Foucault, "Friendship as a Way of Life," trans. John Johnston, in *Foucault Live*, ed. Sylvère Lotringer (New York: Semiotext(e), 1989), 205.

p.39 Edmund White, "Love Stories," review of *To the Friend Who Did Not Save My Life, The Man in The Red Hat, Compassion Protocol*, by Hervé Guibert, *London Review of Books*, November 4, 1993.

p.39 "desire-in-uneasiness": Foucault, "On the Genealogy of Ethics: An Overview of Work in Progress," in *Foucault Reader*, ed. Paul Rabinow, (New York: Pantheon, 1984), 353.

p.45 "That was the last tape of Muzil . . ." *To the Friend*, 27.

p.46 "It must all be considered . . .": Barthes, *Roland Barthes by Roland Barthes*, trans. Richard Howard (Berkeley: University of California Press, 1977), 119.

p.46 Sophie Calle, *Double Game* (London: Violette Editions, 2007).

p.47 I found the essay "Paper Tigress," by Yve-Alain Bois, helpful in his reading of Calle's work and her relationship to other writers, included in *October* 116 (Spring 2006).

p.48 "our adventuress": *To the Friend*, 120.

p.48 "My love, You remember Hervé Guibert?" Sophie Calle, *Exquisite Pain* (New York: Thames and Hudson, 2005), 72.

p.49 "So I decided to play the game." *ibid*, 72.

p.49 "I realized there and then . . ." *ibid*, 72.

p.46 Sophie Calle, Greg Shephard, dir., *Double Blind (No Sex Last Night)* (1992).

p.51 Maurice Blanchot, *The Writing of the Disaster*, trans. Ann Smock (Lincoln: University of Nebraska Press, 2015).

p.52 Eva Hesse, interview with Cindy Nemser, re-diffused as part of *Recording Artists*, Getty Museum, podcast audio, November 11, 2019.

"To Write As If Already Dead" Part Two

p.55 "Studies are often more beautiful . . .": *Compassion*, 92.

p.58 "I had AIDS for three months . . .": *ibid*, 15.

p.58 "a genuine science fiction adventure . . .": *ibid*, 16.

p.59 "several months after those three months . . ." *ibid*, 16.

p.59 "How long have you been under observation?" *To the Friend*, 59.

p.60 "I am alone here and they feel sorry for me . . .": *ibid*, 18.

p.60 Maurice Blanchot, *The Space of Literature*, trans. Ann Smock, (Lincoln: University of Nebraska Press, 2015), 28.

p.60 "I am beginning a new book to have a companion . . ." *To the Friend*, 18.

p.60 "like the plague . . ." *ibid*, 16.

p.60 "These notes link me to my fellow humans . . .": Georges Bataille, *Guilty*, trans. Bruce Boone (Venice, CA: The Lapis Press, 1988), 17.

p.63 "My blood count continues to deteriorate with each passing day . . ." *To the Friend*, 19.

p.63 "the circulatory system . . . a labyrinth": *ibid*, 19.

p.63 "immunological plankton" *ibid*, 20.

p.63 "Someone about to start taking AZT is already dead . . ." *ibid*, 212.

p.64 "Today, January 4, 1989." *ibid*, 53.

p.64 "propelling me publicly into an openly admitted stage of the disease . . ." *ibid*, 53.

p.64 "this borderline of uncertainty . . .": *ibid*, 17.

p.67 "I need solitude for my writing . . .": Franz Kafka, *The Diaries of Franz Kafka* (New York: Vintage Classics, 1999), 17. A quote given to me by Sofia Samatar.

p.67 "friendship's daily bulletins": *To the Friend*, 37.

p.69 "fear and longing": *ibid*, 145.

p.69 "When I am told I am in great shape . . .": *Mausoleum*, 401.

p.70 "famous plague": *To the Friend*, 44.

p.70 "In an instant . . .": *ibid*, 30.

p.70 "undoubtedly imaginary ailments that tormented me": *ibid*, 50.

p.71 "[The office] where he conducted his most titillating experiments": *ibid*, 48.

p.71 "pale, translucent manikin": *ibid*, 51.

p.72 "old whore": *ibid*, 64.

p.72 "That's the chronology that becomes my outline . . .": *ibid*, 63.

p.79 Emily Apter in "Fantom Images: Hervé Guibert and the Writing of 'sida' in France" in *Writing AIDS* makes a useful distinction between *sida* and AIDS, and writes this beautiful description of *To the Friend*: "His novels are neither fiction nor pure autobiography; combining elements of both, they resemble working notebooks dispatched from the land of ghosts.": *Writing AIDS*, ed. James Graham and Mark Wasiuta (New York: Columbia University Press, 1993).

p.74 Bhanu Kapil's blog, first entitled "Was Jack Kerouac a Punjabi?" and later renamed "The Vortex of Formidable Sparkles," is no longer, but she writes brilliantly through notes and blogs in *Ban en Banlieue* (Brooklyn: Nightboat Books, 2015).

p.74 "The novel requires an accumulation of time . . .": César Aira, "Novels Defeat the Law of Diminishing Returns," *The Paris Review* (February 22, 2019). Published originally in *Birthday*, trans. Chris Andrews (New York: New Directions, 2019).

p.75 "You cannot write a novel . . .": *ibid.*

p.75 "It's death that drives me . . .": *Mausoleum*, 51.

p.44 Wayne Koestenbaum cites Guibert as a diarist above all in his *Bookforum* review of the diaries. Wayne Koestenbaum, "The Pleasure of the Text," review of *The Mausoleum of Lovers*, by Hervé Guibert, *Book Forum*, June/July/August, 2014.

p.75 "It is when what I am writing . . .": *Compassion*, 72.

p.77 "that wonderful man . . .": *To the Friend*, 88.

p.77 "Get it into your head I'm not your father!": *ibid*, 88.

p.77 Mathieu Lindon, *Learning What Love Means*, trans. Bruce Benderson (Los Angeles: Semiotext(e), 2017).

p.78 "At some point the writer . . .": Maurice Blanchot, *The Unavowable Community*, trans. Pierre Joris (Barrytown, NY: Station Hill Press, 2006), 46.

p.78 "around the world . . .": *To the Friend*, 60.

p.79 Virginie Despentes, *King Kong Theory*, trans. Stéphanie Benson (New York: The Feminist Press at CUNY, 2010).

p.80 "endlessly multiplying her face.": *To the Friend*, 82.

p.81 "I'd modeled my main character on her": *ibid*, 82.

p.81 "She appeared in a god-awful white dress": *ibid*, 84.

p.81 "Marine looked like a frantic monkey . . .": *ibid*, 80.

p.82 "I myself do not think my books are unkind . . .": *Compassion*, 95–96.

p.83 Audre Lorde, *Zami: A New Spelling of My Name* (Watertown, MA: Persephone, 1982).

p.83 Guibert, "Ghost Image," 13.

p.85 "it is perhaps preferable to circle around . . .": *Mausoleum*, 188.

p.87   "My book is battling the fatigue . . .": *To the Friend*, 69.

p.87   "He understood there was no way to escape Time . . .": Chris Marker, dir. *La jetée*. (Paris: RTF, 1962), DVD.

p.89   Italo Calvino, *Six Memos for the Next Millennium (The Charles Eliot Norton Lectures, 1985–86)*, trans. Patrick Creagh (New York: Vintage, 1993).

p.89   ". . . when I learned I was going to die": *To the Friend*, 72.

p.91   ". . . an Auschwitzian exhibit" *Compassion*, 6.

p.91   Elizabeth Wurtzel, "The Breast Cancer Gene and Me," *The New York Times*, September 25, 2015.

p.94   Reading Andrew Durbin's foreword to the reissue made me more aware of the history of the Institut Alfred-Fournier as a hospital for treating syphilis patients. Andrew Durbin, "A Guide for Living," in Hervé Guibert, *To the Friend Who Did Not Save My Life*, trans. Linda Coverdale (Los Angeles: Semiotext(e), 2020).

p.94   "that when this certainty became official . . ." *To the Friend*, 143.

p.95   "new complicities, new tenderness, new solidarities" *ibid*, 35.

p.95   "still my love for them was a potential bloodbath . . ." *ibid*, 200.

p.95   "They are like escalating fevers, outbursts.": *Apostrophes*, "Hervé Guibert 'A l'ami qui ne m'a pas sauvé la vie'," trans. Philo Cohen. *INA Archives* video, March 16, 1991.

p.95   "a work of imitative fiction that is . . .": *To the Friend*, 204.

p.95   Thomas Bernhard, *Extinction*, trans. David McLintock. (New York: Vintage, 2011).

p.96   ". . . fake, disguised essays . . .": *To the Friend*, 205.

p.96   "Often when I write a book . . .": *Apostrophes*.

p.96   "I'd have to choose between . . .": *To the Friend*, 30.

p.97   "I'd add those seventy drops . . .": *ibid*, 206.

p.98   "Here is what I did with my body one day . . ." Barthes, *Roland Barthes by Roland Barthes*, 61.

p.98   "rib chop" *ibid*, 61.

p.98   "this fragment of myself" *ibid*, 61.

p.99   Michel Leiris, *Manhood*, trans. Richard Howard (Chicago: University of Chicago Press, 1992).

p.99 "It's the dead ballet dancer's DDI . . .": *Compassion*, 69.

p.99 "I was alive again . . ." *ibid*, 43.

p.99 Eve Kosofsky Sedgwick, "Introduction," in *Touching Feeling: Affect, Pedagogy, Performativity*, (Durham, NC: Duke University Press, 2003), 13.

p.100 "little blond curly-haired masseur": *To the Friend*, 62.

p.100 "Yet at the same time, we were all catching the disease from one another's bodies . . ." *ibid*, 62.

p.100 "mutual massacre": *ibid*, 195.

p.100 "repellent specter": *ibid*, 150.

p.100 "reciprocal recontamination": *ibid*, 150.

p.100 "And we both knew that Jules couldn't live": *ibid*, 150.

p.101 "This attempt at fucking struck me right away as unspeakably sad . . .": *ibid*, 151.

p.101 "even when he'd begged me to treat him like a slut . . .": *ibid*, 154.

p.101 "godless, lawless murderers": *ibid*, 154.

p.102 "I think the pleasures these children give me are greater than the ones of the flesh . . ." *ibid*, 201.

p.102 Guibert, *Crazy for Vincent*, trans. Christine Pichini (Los Angeles: Semiotext(e), 2017).

p.102 Moyra Davey, *Burn the Diaries* (Brooklyn: Dancing Foxes Press, 2014).

p.103 "a searching, moral voice . . .": David Velasco, "Introduction," in David Wojnarowicz, *Weight of The Earth: The Tape Journals of David Wojnarowicz* (Los Angeles: Semiotext(e), 2018), 11.

p.104 "nothing more than just another infected little faggot . . ." *Compassion*, 47.

p.104 "alone on the paper-sheeted table . . .": *ibid*, 48.

p.104 "I had become incapable of recounting . . .": *ibid*, 48.

p.104 "Muzil spent a morning in the hospital . . .": *To the Friend*, 36.

p.107 "relishing the moments of sweet humanity": *ibid*, 219. Moyra Davey's reading of the ending of *To the Friend* made me newly aware of the "beauty and tenderness" of the sections narrating the weekly trips to the Spallanzani Clinic in Rome. (Davey, *Burn the Diaries*, 30.)

p.109 Eve Kosofsky Sedgwick, "Paranoid Reading and Reparative Reading; or, You're So Paranoid, You Probably Think This Introduction is About You", in *Touching Feeling: Affect, Pedagogy, Performativity*, (Durham: Duke University Press, 2003), 123.

p.109 Sedgwick, "Paranoid Reading and Reparative Reading; or, You're So Paranoid, You Probably Think This Introduction is About You", 128.

p.110 "death's head": *To the Friend*, 58.

p.110 "cadaverous": *ibid*, 228.

p.112 "There is the recurring question . . .": *Apostrophes*.

p.113 "the well-polished bare bones.": *To the Friend*, 97.

p.113 "some vulture": *ibid*, 104.

p.113 "Yes it's awful but it's the truth": *Apostrophes*.

p.113 "I was writing intolerable things . . .": *ibid*.

p.114 "I knew that Muzil would have been so hurt . . .": *To the Friend*, 96.

p.114 "The sister had demanded . . ." *ibid*, 109.

p.115 "punishment for a person's transgression": Susan Sontag, "AIDS and Its Metaphors," in *Illness as Metaphor and AIDS and Its Metaphors*, (New York: Picador, 1988), 102.

p.115-116 "new complicities, new tenderness, new solidarities" *To the Friend*, 35.

p.116 "closet queen": *Apostrophes*

p.116 "calling out the names written there . . .": *To the Friend*, 58.

p.116 "Later I wondered if he'd said that intentionally . . .": *ibid*, 57.

p.116 "Like Muzil, I would have liked . . .": *ibid*, 21.

p.116 "I felt death approaching in the mirror . . ." *ibid*, 21.

p.118 "calm the imagination, not incite it.": Sontag, "AIDS and Its Metaphors," 102.

p.118 "classic script for plague," *ibid*, 139.

p.125 "I'm actually writing all of this on the evening . . .": *ibid*, 53.

p.125 "It is ambivalent. It is pregnant death, a death that gives birth." Mikhail Bakhtin, *Rabelais and His World* (Bloomington: Indiana University Press, 1984), 25.

p.125 Durbin, "A Guide for Living", 8.

p.125   "With semisheer stockings and flats . . .": *To the Friend*, 164.

p.127   "a phantom hospital at the end of the earth": *ibid*, 54.

p.127   "The nurse who was supposed to . . .": *ibid*, 59.

p.127   Wojnarowicz, "Living Close to The Knives," in *Close to the Knives: A Memoir of Disintegration*, (New York: Vintage, 1991), 114

p.128   Julia Kristeva, "Powers of Horror," in *Powers of Horror: An Essay on Abjection*, trans. Leon S. Roudiez (New York: Columbia University Press, 1982), 207–211.

p.131   Bernhard, *Wittgenstein's Nephew*, trans. David McLintock (New York: Vintage, 2009).

p.133   "When I got the proofs I had doubts . . .": Antoine de Gaudemar, "Les aveux permanents d' Herve Guibert," trans. Jean Pierre Boulé, *Liberation*, October 20, 1988, in Jean Pierre Boulé, *Hervé Guibert: Voices of Self* (Liverpool: Liverpool University Press, 1999), 193.

p.134   David Velasco writes about David Wojnarowicz as a saint in his introduction to the Tape Journals.

p.134   "individual adventure": Didier Lestrade, "Against Guibert" (Paris: Editions Denoël, 2000), trans. Benjamin Gagnon Chainey in "The People of Act Up Paris Against Hervé Guibert," *Synapsis*, February 2, 2018.

p.134   Wojnarowicz, "Living Close to The Knives," 99.

p.138   "Just as AIDS will have been my paradigm in my project of self-revelation . . ." *To the Friend*, 233.

p.139   "But he was tired, and so was I . . ." *ibid*, 194.

p.138   Mathieu Lindon talks about this as the original title of the novel in his memoir, as mentioned in Andrew Durbin's introduction to the reissue.

p.139   "My book is closing in on me . . ." *To the Friend*, 251.

p.141   "I'm no superstar shit and never will be. . . ." Kathy Acker, "Kathy Acker by Mark Magill," BOMB, 1983.

p.141   "Thinking takes time . . .": Etel Adnan, *Surge* (Brooklyn: Nightboat Books, 2018), 30.

p.141   Guibert, dir., *La Pudeur et l'impudeur*, (Paris: TF1, 1992), DVD.